Easy Peasy Language Arts 3 Parent's Guide

Welcome to the EP Language Arts 3 Parent's Guide!

This little book was created to help you go offline while following EP's Language Arts 3 curriculum. You will need the Language Arts 3 Workbook for your child. Without the online lessons, you will need to be your child's teacher. The directions are here for introducing new topics. The workbook will provide practice and review.

This book also includes objectives for each lesson, materials marked where needed, directions for what to do each lesson, and the complete answer key.

This course covers all language arts topics including writing, grammar, handwriting, and spelling. Throughout the year, students will be writing creatively as well as writing non-fiction as they learn to construct paragraphs.

Each lesson's instruction ends with the worksheet, so if you haven't gotten there yet, please continue onto the next page.

A little note: To avoid calling all children "he" or the awkward phrasing of "him or her," I've used the plural pronoun when referring to your child, such as, "Brainstorm with your child words that rhyme with tree, and see how many they can come up with."

Have a great year,

Lee

Lesson 1

- Students will: practice their personal information
- Lesson 1 worksheet
  - They just need to write their name, address, and phone number.

Lesson 2

- Students will: identify repetition in poetry
- Lesson 2 worksheet
  - They will copy lines of poetry with repetition.

Lesson 3

- Students will: copy lines of poetry that are repeated in the poems
- There wasn't room on their page for today's poems. Why not read them to your child? They will be copying some of the first lines of the stanzas. They repeat each time but with little differences. The repeated patterns are a poetic technique.
  - *Laughing Song* by William Blake

    When the green woods laugh with the voice of joy,
    And the dimpling stream runs laughing by;
    When the air does laugh with our merry wit,
    And the green hill laughs with the noise of it;

    When the meadows laugh with lively green,
    And the grasshopper laughs in the merry scene;
    When Mary and Susan and Emily
    With their sweet round mouths sing 'Ha ha he!'

    When the painted birds laugh in the shade,
    Where our table with cherries and nuts is spread:
    Come live, and be merry, and join with me,
    To sing the sweet chorus of 'Ha ha he!'

  - A Cradle Song by William Blake

    Sweet dreams, form a shade
    O'er my lovely infant's head!
    Sweet dreams of pleasant streams
    By happy, silent, moony beams!

    Sweet Sleep, with soft down
    Weave thy brows an infant crown!
    Sweet Sleep, angel mild,
    Hover o'er my happy child!

Sweet smiles, in the night
Hover over my delight!
Sweet smiles, mother's smiles,
All the livelong night beguiles.

Sweet moans, dovelike sighs,
Chase not slumber from thy eyes!
Sweet moans, sweeter smiles,
All the dovelike moans beguiles.

Sleep, sleep, happy child!
All creation slept and smiled.
Sleep, sleep, happy sleep,
While o'er thee thy mother weep.

Sweet babe, in thy face
Holy image I can trace;
Sweet babe, once like thee
Thy Maker lay, and wept for me:

Wept for me, for thee, for all,
When He was an infant small.
Thou His image ever see,
Heavenly face that smiles on thee!

Smiles on thee, on me, on all,
Who became an infant small;
Infant smiles are His own smiles;
Heaven and earth to peace beguiles.

- Lesson 3 worksheet
  - They will copy the lines of poetry.

Lesson 4

- Students will: copy a stanza of a poem
- Lesson 4 worksheet
  - They will copy a poem paying attention to its structure.

Lesson 5

- Students will: write a poem
- Lesson 5 worksheet
  - They will write a poem using repetition.

Lesson 6

- Students will: practice spelling, alphabetize, identify synonyms and antonyms, identify plurals, count syllables
- Look at the worksheet to talk about what they need to do.
  - The first question requires students to put words in alphabetical order.
    - Does your child know the order of the alphabet?
    - Ask your child which word comes first in alphabetical order, apple or banana?
    - A comes before B in the alphabet, so a word starting with A comes before a word that starts with B in alphabetical order.
    - They can fill it in now, or you can ask them to wait until you talk about the different parts first.
  - Ask your child how many syllables apple and banana have.
    - Clap together to figure it out.
    - "Other words" is just the middle section.
  - A synonym is a word of similar meaning.
    - What word means nigh or close?
      - near
  - An antonym is a word of opposite meaning.
    - What word means the opposite of low?
      - high
  - Ask your child what a plural word is.
    - when there is more than one
- Lesson 6 worksheet
  - Read over the short A / short E section together and remind your child of what the short sound is of those vowels, such as in hat and bed.
  - They should check off the words as they use them to find what's left over.
  - Then they will write a sentence using a verb from the list.

Lesson 7

- Students will: write rhymes and alliteration
- Together think of rhyming pairs of words. Rhyming words end with the same sound.
  - Examples: sweet feet, low blow, free bee, bite fright, etc.
- Together think of alliteration pairs. Alliteration is when words begin with the same sound.
  - Examples: corn cob, dark day, fancy feet, tickle toes, etc.
- Lesson 7 worksheet
  - They will write twenty words: five pairs of rhymes and five pairs of alliteration.

Lesson 8

- Students will: write a poem by counting syllables
- Practice counting syllables. Clap with each syllable as you say the words.
  - pea-nut but-ter

- o re-en-act-ment
- o be-lieve
- o beau-ti-ful
- o Try your names.
- Read these stanzas of this poem to your child and clap syllables together. It's William Blake's, "The Fly." Read each line and then repeat with clapping.

> Little Fly,
> Thy summer's play
> My thoughtless hand
> Has brushed away.
> …
> Then am I
> A happy fly.
> If I live,
> Or if I die.

- Lesson 8 worksheet
    - o They will write a poem with the rhythm of three syllables on the first line and then four syllables on the next three lines.
    - o It doesn't matter what it says really. It can just be nonsense. The point is the syllable count.
    - o I wrote an example on their page. Can they find the rhyme? Their poem doesn't have to rhyme.

Lesson 9

- Students will: write an acrostic poem
- Lesson 9 worksheet
    - o Write the current month down the workbook page, one letter per line. You can certainly choose a different month if you like. They will have to write a word on each line that begins with the letter on that line.
    - o There is a partial example on the page.

Lesson 10

- Students will: write a theme poem
- Lesson 10 worksheet
    - o They will write a poem about an apple. Brainstorm together words about apples.
        - ▪ red, yellow, green, sweet, sour, trees, fall, crunch, delicious, juicy, etc.
    - o Their poem can be a list of words or done in sentences. (ie. I like to eat apples. They are…)

Lesson 11

- Students will: write a rhyming rhythmic poem with alliteration, put words in alphabetical order, identify plurals
- They are to write two lines of poetry today. The lines are to rhyme, and they are to have the same number of syllables. The last instruction is to include alliteration.
  - Here's my example. Below it I'll walk you through creating a similar poem.
    - My dog's name is Mighty Max
    - He leaves behind muddy tracks
      - Mighty Max is alliteration.
      - Max and tracks rhyme.
      - Each line has 7 syllables.
  - Start with the alliteration. Remind your child that alliteration is when you have at least two words in a row that begin with the same sound.
    - Have your child come up with an alliteration to use in their poem.
      - examples: tall trees, big boat, cold camp, slithering snake
  - Next, have your child put that in a sentence. This can be the first line of their poem.
    - examples: I like to climb tall trees. I once rode on a big boat. We spent the night at the cold camp. I don't want to step on that slithering snake.
  - Count up the syllables in their sentence.
    - examples: 6, 7, 8, 11 (from my example sentences)
  - Now think up words that rhyme with the last word in their sentence.
    - examples: bees, please…coat, vote…damp, lamp…bake, lake… (from my example sentences)
  - Put that rhyming word at the end of a sentence.
  - Count up the syllables in your rhyming sentence. It needs to have the same number as the first sentence to create a certain rhythm for your poem. Do you need to take out or add syllables?
  - Figure out your sentence and write the two poem lines on the worksheet.
- Lesson 11 worksheet
  - There is also a spelling activity on this page. Read over the short I/O/U words together and remind your child what the short vowel sound is of each vowel as in hit, hot, and hut. This is mainly to practice the terminology of long and short vowels.
  - They've seen the spelling activities before. Do they remember alphabetical order and plural words?
    - To put words in alphabetical order you start with their first letter and compare where they come in the alphabet.
    - Plural words are words that show there are more than one: one book, two books.

Lesson 12

- Students will: write a poem
- They are to write a poem about the month you are in.
  - Brainstorm together about the month. You could write the words they come up with on their worksheet. (This will help them with their spelling while they are writing their poem. Spelling and grammar aren't the focus of these writing activities. You don't want them dampening any creativity.)
    - What's it like? Think of descriptive words: cold, warm, sunny, gray, rainy, breezy…
    - Think of things that happen in this month: holidays, birthdays, events…
    - Think of things you did or will do this month: visiting, trips, friends,…
  - Ask your child what poetry technique they want to try: repetition, alliteration, rhyming, or rhythm. (They can use more than one!)
    - If they choose alliteration or rhyme, brainstorm together using the words and ideas you just came up with.
- Lesson 12 worksheet
  - They will write a poem. It should be at least two lines, but encourage four at least. It does not have to rhyme, but praise your child for any rhyme, rhythm, or alliteration used.

Lesson 13

- Students will: write a descriptive poem
- They are going to write a poem about a sunset.
  - Brainstorm words related to a sunset. You could write them on lines on their worksheet. What colors are in a sunset? When do you see a sunset? What do you feel when you see a sunset? (My answers aren't the "right" answers, just examples.)
    - orange, red; evening, end of the day; peaceful, rest, inspiring
  - Ask your child what poem technique they'd like to use: repetition, alliteration, rhythm, or rhyme.
    - Brainstorm together ideas for their poem using their choice. Orange does not rhyme!
- Lesson 13 worksheet

Lesson 14

- Students will: write a rhyming rhythmic poem
- They are to write two lines of poetry that rhyme. Each line should have eight syllables.
  - You can start with two rhyming words. You can write these down on their worksheet.
  - Have your child work at putting them into lines with 8 syllables.
    - Here's an example.
      - I like to climb *very* tall trees. (I added very to make it longer. Use descriptive words to make your sentences longer.)

- I like to climb up in the breeze.
    - I used repetition: "I like to climb."
- Lesson 14 worksheet

Lesson 15

- Students will: write a poem using descriptive words
- Lesson 15 worksheet
    - Look at the worksheet together. Read the words together.
    - They are to use those words to create a poem. They just need to order the words.

Lesson 16

- Students will write a poem with descriptive language, practice spelling
- Have your child choose their favorite color.
    - Brainstorm together things that are that color.
    - They are going to be writing a poem of metaphors.
        - Red tastes like apple.
        - Red smells like fire.
        - Red feels like a bumpy strawberry.
        - Red looks like a heart in love.
        - Red sounds like a fire truck.
- Lesson 16 worksheet
    - On their page, have your child write (or write this part for them if writing is hard) their chosen color on each line followed by one of the senses: tastes, smells, feels, looks, sounds. It will look like the example I just gave with red.
        - Then they can put in things of that color that go best with each sense.
    - The bottom part of the page is spelling.
        - Have them read you the words. Point out the long vowel sounds this time and where a silent E makes the vowel say its name. When a vowel says its name, it's called a long vowel.
        - They need to find words with more than one syllable, words with a silent E at the end, and words with vowel pairs in the middle, which means words that have two vowels next to each other.
            - Vowels are A E I O U.
        - They need to use each word only once, so it can be helpful to check off words they have already used.

Lesson 17

- Students will: write a biographical poem
- Lesson 17 worksheet
    - There are instructions on the page. Read them together. This does not have to have rhythm or rhyme. They are just expressing themselves.

Lesson 18

- Students will: write a rhythmic rhyming list poem
- Shel Silverstein has a famous list poem called, "Sick." The child says they can't go to school and lists all the things wrong with them. Then the child learns it's Saturday and jumps out of bed just fine.
- Here's the start of another famous list poem. It's *Bleezer's Ice Cream* by Jack Prelutsky.
  - o I am Ebenezer Bleezer,
    I run BLEEZER'S ICE CREAM STORE,
    there are flavors in my freezer
    you have never seen before,
    twenty-eight divine creations
    too delicious to resist,
    why not do yourself a favor,
    try the flavors on my list:

    COCOA MOCHA MACARONI
    TAPIOCA SMOKED BALONEY…
  - o It continues with lots of silly pairs of rhyming flavors.
- Have your child think about what they want to list for their poem: maybe foods, activities, games, people, toys, places, etc.
  - o Together brainstorm a list of rhyming words in the category they choose. You can write those on their page.
  - o There are 8 lines on their page. If you write on two, they can write three pairs of rhyming lines for their poem.
- Lesson 18 worksheet
  - o They can write a short introduction to their list: I went to visit, I had for dinner, I bought at the store, or they can use the example opening on their worksheet page and go from there.
  - o Then, they can start their list. Each pair of lines can rhyme. There can be other words in between the rhyming words. Here's an example.
    - ▪ I bought chips and juice and a pound of ground beef,
      crackers and pickles and one lettuce leaf.
  - o Have them read it out loud to listen for rhythm. The lines should be about the same length to give it rhythm. Together you can note places where it doesn't sound right and add a word or take out a word to get the rhythm flowing better.

Lesson 19

- Students will: write a poem about a flower
- Lesson 19 worksheet
  - o Brainstorm words about flowers.
    - ▪ You or your child could write them in the petals.
  - o Then your child can take those words and make a poem. It doesn't have to have rhyme or rhythm. You can refer back to the color poem (Lesson 16) for inspiration. A flower is… A flower smells like… A flower feels like…

Lesson 20

- Students will: write a poem
- Lesson 20 worksheet
  - There are no directions for today. There is space for a picture. They can list words. They can rhyme. They can be minimalists. They can write a pretty poem about rainbows or a silly poem about their stinky feet.

Lesson 21

- Students will: practice spelling, write an exclamatory sentence
- Lesson 21 worksheet
  - They need to follow the directions on the page to write each word once in the blanks. Read through the long vowel words together to practice recognizing the difference between long and short vowels.
  - They should check off the words they have used to make it easier.
  - The bottom of the page is a sentence they are to write using one of the verbs listed. It should end in an exclamation point. It should be an exciting or loud sentence!

Lesson 22

- Students will: copy morals from Aesop's Fables
- Lesson 22 worksheet
  - They can choose from the morals listed on their page. Give them a high five and/or hug if they fill all the lines by writing more than required.

Lesson 23

- Students will: alphabetize words
- Lesson 23 worksheet
  - Quick and easy today…They just need to number the words in alphabetical order. They will compare the first letter of each word to decide which comes first, second, third, and last.

Lesson 24

- Students will: write a story with a moral
- The moral your child will be teaching through their story today is look before you leap. Ask your child what they think it means.
  - It means to not rush into things. Consider the outcome and risks before you start something.
  - You could leap off a cliff and there may be nowhere to land!
  - See if your child can come up with an example of someone not looking before they leap.

- Lesson 24 worksheet
  - There is a story starter on the page that your child could use if they don't have their own idea. You can read the starter and talk about ideas.

Lesson 25

- Students will: share their wisdom, alphabetize words
- Lesson 25 worksheet
  - They need to come up with a moral or a lesson they want others to know. They can use Aesop's morals for inspiration.
  - There are a couple of alphabetizing activities on the bottom of the page they can do quickly. They are similar to the ones in Lesson 23.

Lesson 26

- Students will: practice spelling, alphabetical order, counting syllables
- Lesson 26 worksheet
  - Look over the directions about consonants, syllables, and alphabetical order. Make sure your child is confident about what to look for.
    - Consonants are everything other than the vowels (AEIOU)
    - Clap to count the syllables in a word.
    - To check alphabetical order, look at the first letter in the word.
  - Remind your child to check off the words as they are used. Each word is used only once.

Lesson 27

- Students will: practice curiosity, write questions, use question marks, find answers
- Curiosity is the most effective way to learn. When you are curious, your brain gets a reward when it finds the answer, making you want to learn more.
- Lesson 27 worksheet
  - They are to write three questions, but those questions should be ones they want to know the answer to.
  - They will need to find the answers to their questions. It would be fun if they could ask people who know the answers. It would then become a good exercise in asking questions as well.

Lesson 28

- Students will: put words in alphabetical order
- This alphabetical order exercise is more complicated. They will have to look past the first letter.
  - Ask your child what comes first in alphabetical order: ask or ant?

ASK   ANT

- They both start with A.

- When they can't tell from the first letter, they need to look at the next letter.
    - What two letters come after the A?
        - S and N
        - Which comes first in alphabetical order?
            - N
                - So, ant comes before ask in alphabetical order.
- Try it again with these two words.

SHIP   SHAPE

- Ask your child if you can tell the answer by the first letters.
    - No
- What about the second letters?
    - No, they are the same too.
- Ask your child how they will figure out which comes first in alphabetical order.
    - They will compare the I and A.
    - A comes first so shape comes before ship in alphabetical order.
- Lesson 28 worksheet
    - They are to number the words to show their alphabetical order.

Lesson 29

- Students will: practice capitalization
- Ask your child if they remember what words need to be capitalized (which ones need to start with a capital letter).
    - The first letter of any sentence
    - Names: names of people, names of places, names of things, names of months, names of the days of the week,…
    - You can remind your child that all the words of a name need to be capitalized. You can give your street name as an example. Road, Street, Avenue, etc. are part of the street name and are capitalized. You can also use your child's full name as an example. You capitalize the first, middle, and last name. They are all part of your child's name.
- Lesson 29 worksheet
    - They just need to find the words that need to be capitalized.

Lesson 30

- Students will: practice spelling
- Lesson 30 worksheet
    - They just need to copy the words.

Lesson 31

- Students will: practice spelling
- Lesson 31 worksheet
  - Make sure your child remembers what a synonym and antonym are: words of similar and opposite meaning, respectively.
  - Words with a silent E have an E at the end of the word, but you don't say its sound. Words like game, late, and table all have a silent letter E.
  - They will also have to write a sentence with a pronoun.
    - Pronouns are words we use to replace nouns. Use your child's name as an example. "You are doing your work," instead of, "_____ is doing her work."

Lesson 32

- Students will: identify contractions and their meanings
- A contraction is where we shorten words using an apostrophe. Instead of, "I cannot go," we say, "I can't go."
  - Have your child try substituting in a contraction.
    - I am ready. I'm ready.
    - It is so cute. It's so cute.
- Lesson 32 worksheet
  - They will copy the sentence, identify the contraction, write its meaning, and then do it again with their own contraction.

Lesson 33

- Students will: practice commas in a series
- Teach your child about commas in a series.
  - Whenever there are three or more of something in a list, they need to be separated by commas. The final comma goes before the "and" or "or."
    - I always teach to add the comma before the "and." It is not always necessary, but it's not wrong to have it. Since sometimes it's really necessary, I think it's smarter to practice using it.
    - They DO NOT put a comma after the last word in the series.
  - Here are some examples. Ask your child what the list is and where the commas would go.
    - Please bring tape, scissors, paper, and a ruler.
    - I'd take the purple, red, blue, green, or yellow one.
    - The puppies were running, jumping, and yapping.
- Lesson 33 worksheet
  - They will just need to add the commas where words are in lists. A couple of sentences have more than one series in them.

Lesson 34

- Students will: write a dialogue
- The writing prompt on their page is about what they would ask and tell their grandfather if it was the first time they were seeing him. You can talk about that with your child. If they have a different conversation they want to write, that's okay.
- Lesson 34 worksheet
  - Look at the worksheet together to see what format it should be in. Each time the next person talks, it should start on a new line.
  - In Lesson 35, they will rewrite this with quotation marks.

Lesson 35

- Students will: write a dialogue with quotation marks
- Take a look at the worksheet for Lesson 35 together. Point out the comma after "hi" and how "asked" is lower case.
  - They will leave any question marks and exclamation points, but will replace periods with commas like in the example.
  - They will also need to write who said what. That is part of the sentence. That's why "asked" is lower case. It's still part of the same sentence.
  - What the people say will start with a capital letter.
- Lesson 35 worksheet
  - They are rewriting their dialogue with quotation marks. Each time the next person speaks, it should be written on the next line.
  - This is a first attempt, so just encourage them to use the example and try their best. It doesn't have to be perfect.

Lesson 36

- Students will: learn about homophones, practice spelling
- A homophone is a word that sounds like another but is spelled differently.
  - Here are some examples.
    - read/red, hair/hare, bear/bare
    - On their spelling page they will have to look for a homophone. It sounds the same but is spelled differently.
- Lesson 36 worksheet
  - They will need to know homophones, antonyms, and how to figure out the number of syllables.

Lesson 37

- Students will: copy a sentence, practice using commas and capitalization, identify proper nouns, identify words needing to be capitalized
- Lesson 37 worksheet
  - They will copy the two sentences carefully.
    - When they are done, have your child check to see if they used two commas and two capital letters.

- o There is a small capitalization activity on the bottom of the page. The directions remind them that each sentence begins with a capital letter and that every name needs to be capitalized.
  - ▪ If they are unsure, you can give them this clue. The first has three words that need to be capitalized; the next has four; the last has five.

Lesson 38

- Students will: identify correct sentences, practice test taking
- Lesson 38 worksheet
  - o They need to spot the correct sentence. They should pay attention to capitalization and punctuation.
  - o To mark the correct answer they will fill in the circle by the sentence.

Lesson 39

- Students will: write a short story
- Lesson 39 worksheet
  - o There is a writing prompt on the page about a day spent on the mountain. You can talk together about what they saw (pretend), what they smelled, what they did.
  - o Have your child read over the final story and check for capitalization, punctuation, and spelling mistakes.
    - ▪ It's a good habit to develop to always read out loud what you wrote. If a word looks weird, they should ask about it or look it up to make sure it is spelled correctly.
  - o Create a final draft to save.

Lesson 40

- Students will: edit sentences for correct punctuation and capitalization
- Lesson 40 worksheet
  - o They will look for commas, ending punctuation, and contractions that need apostrophes.
  - o They will look for a capital letter at the beginning of each sentence and for all proper nouns to have a capital letter.

Lesson 41

- Students will: practice spelling, alphabetizing, antonyms, synonyms, writing
- Lesson 41 worksheet
  - o They are to write a sentence in command form. Have your child tell you what to do to practice the command form.
  - o Make sure they remember synonyms are words of similar meaning and antonyms are words of opposite meaning.

Lesson 42

- Students will: practice punctuation and capitalization, begin using apostrophes for possessives
- Ask your child what words should be capitalized.
    - First letter in every sentence and proper nouns, which are the names of people, places, and things.
- Ask your child when they need to use a comma.
    - They have learned about using commas in a series to separate words in a list.
- Ask your child to tell you something that belongs to them, the book for instance. Use your child's name to say it as a possessive, for instance: Lee's book.
    - Try it with some other objects.
    - Write one or more of them down to show the 's.
    - We use an apostrophe and S to show possession (that someone has something). You don't have to teach this rule now, but if your child happens to have a name that ends in S, then you just add the apostrophe. No S is needed because it already has one.
- Lesson 42 worksheet
    - They have two sentences to copy. Remind them to only capitalize the letters that are supposed to be capitalized. There are also commas that they should be careful to copy.
    - On the bottom part of the page, they just need to circle the letters that should be capitalized and draw in the missing punctuation. There are commas, an apostrophe, and ending punctuation to fill in.

Lesson 43

- Students will: edit sentences correcting apostrophes, commas, ending punctuation, and capitalization errors
- Lesson 43 worksheet
    - This is a practice of what they've already been doing this week. Encourage them to use the clues to find what they are missing instead of telling them the answer.

Lesson 44

- Students will: write a creative story
- Lesson 44 worksheet
    - The writing prompt is about a day in the big city. You could talk first to brainstorm ideas.
    - This is one you could write for your child if it's hard for them to physically write.
    - When your child is done, have them read it out loud. If they notice anything wrong, they should fix it.

Lesson 45

- Students will: practice quotation marks
- Ask your child if they remember what quotation marks are for.
  - They show us someone is speaking.
- Lesson 45 worksheet
  - They will copy a quote and write that Abraham Lincoln said it. They need to use a comma and quotation marks.

Lesson 46

- Students will: practice spelling, identify long and short vowel sounds, alphabetize
- Ask your child if they remember the difference between long and short vowels.
- Lesson 46 worksheet
  - Take a look at this together. Have your child look at the first column. Five have silent Es but only one has a long vowel sound: stage.
    - Engine looks like it should, but it breaks the spelling rules.
    - Have your child figure out why the E doesn't make the others have a long vowel sound.
      - There are two letters between the vowel and the E. That keeps the vowels apart, so the E doesn't affect the vowel.

Lesson 47

- Students will: identify parts of a letter, identify the correct way to use parts of a letter
- They are going to be learning about letter writing.
  - There are five parts to a letter. Read this list and find each part in the example below. Notice where the capital letters and the commas belong.
    - The <u>heading</u> is your address and/or the date.
    - The <u>salutation</u> is the greeting: Hello, or Dear so and so. It starts with a capital letter and is followed by a comma.
    - The <u>body</u> is the information you are sending in the letter, what you want to tell the person. Follow all the normal rules of writing.
    - The <u>closing</u> is how you close your letter. We say things like: sincerely, yours truly, blessings, thinking of you, and a number of other words or short phrases. The closing starts with a capital letter and is followed by a comma just like the salutation.
    - The <u>signature</u> is your name.

March 11, 2017

Dear Mr. Pickle,

I hope this letter finds you well, and you aren't still sour.

Sincerely,

Mr. Gherkin

- Lesson 47 worksheet
    - They will be choosing the correct punctuation and capitalization for each of these sections.

Lesson 48

- Students will: edit sentences for correct usage
- Before they tackle the worksheet, practice with object pronouns.
    - The easiest way to know which pronoun to use is to take out any name used. Here are examples:
        - Piper and me sang together today.
            - Would you say me sang today?
                - No, you would say I sang, so the correct sentence is Piper and I sang together today.
        - Can you give those to William and I?
            - Would you say give those to I?
                - No, you would say give those to me, so the correct sentence is can you give those to William and me.
    - They will also be choosing the correct verb. A verb tense tells us when the action happened.
        - Run is the present tense. If someone is running, they are doing it right now.
        - Ran is the past tense. If someone ran, they already did it. They aren't doing it now.
- Lesson 48 worksheet – Encourage your child to read the sentences out loud. It will help them hear the mistakes.

Lesson 49

- Students will: write a friendly letter
    - Turn to Lesson 47 in the workbook and review the parts of a letter. Remind your child how the salutation and closing begin with a capital letter and end with a comma.

- Lesson 49 worksheet
  - They will write a letter. They can write any letter, but there is a prompt on the page about writing to your grandfather (or from Heidi to her grandfather). The body of the letter can just be a sentence, but make sure they use all five parts of a letter correctly.

Lesson 50

- Students will: identify root words in words with prefixes and suffixes
- A prefix is a part added onto the beginning of a word to change its meaning.
  - We can change the root word believable into unbelievable by adding the prefix, UN.
  - Think together about what other words have the prefix UN. What do they mean with and without the prefix?
    - tie, untie
    - able, unable
    - helpful, unhelpful
      - When you add on UN, the word means the opposite. UN means not.
- A suffix is a part added onto the end of a word to change its meaning.
  - We can add ABLE onto words to say that it can be done.
    - We can change believe into believable.
      - That means it's able to be believed.
    - We can change understand into understandable.
      - That means it's able to be understood.
    - Can you think of any other examples?
      - countable
      - touchable
      - reliable
- What would untouchable mean? What's the root word?
  - The root word is touch. UN means not and ABLE means able, so it means not able to be touched.
- Lesson 50 worksheet
  - Create words by combining root words with prefixes and suffixes.
  - They just need to circle the answers.

Lesson 51

- Students will: understand the meanings of root words and prefixes
- Lesson 51 worksheet
  - They will use each prefix and each root word once, so they should tick off what they use.
  - Encourage them to fill in the ones they are sure of first and then come back to ones they aren't sure of. Also, reading the root and prefix pairs out loud will help them find matches.

Lesson 52

- Students will: write a friendly letter
- Turn to the workbook page for Lesson 49 and look at the letter. Have your child point out the heading, salutation, body, closing, and signature. Point out how the heading and closing both start with a capital letter and are followed by a comma.
- Lesson 52 worksheet
  - They are to write a letter. The important part is the form of the letter. The body doesn't have to be more than one or two sentences.

Lesson 53

- Students will: edit sentences to correct capitalization and punctuation
- Ask your child what words need to be capitalized.
  - first word in each sentence
  - names of people, places, and things
    - that includes names of months and names of the days of the week
- They will be looking for lists where they will put commas between the words in a series.
- They will also need to add apostrophes. Ask your child where those are used.
  - They are used in contractions turning *I am* into *I'm* and *cannot* into *can't*.
  - They are also used to show possession (that something belongs to someone), as in Mary's child and the dog's collar.
- Lesson 53 worksheet
  - They are to underline the words that need capital letters and add in missing punctuation. There are clues on the page.

Lesson 54

- Students will: write a business letter
- They can write to the publishers of Heidi if they are reading that right now for school. Otherwise, they can choose any favorite book.
- The form of a business letter starts with your name and address and date in the top right corner.
- Under that on the left is the name/title of the person you are sending your letter to and their address.
- Next comes the salutation. For a business letter this takes a different form. You still start with a capital letter. You can write, "To Whom It May Concern." It is followed by a colon instead of a comma. To Whom It May Concern:
- Then there is the body. They can write about their favorite thing about the book and that they are happy it was published. They can even make suggestions. How would they end the book?
- Finally there is a closing and signature. These follow the same guidelines as for a friendly letter except you'd need to make sure to write your full name.

- Lesson 54 worksheet
    - The page is set up for your child to fill in the letter format. Help your child with your own address and today's date on the right.
    - You can address it to the publisher on the left. For Heidi it's: Grosset & Dunlap Publishers, 345 Hudson Street 10th Floor, New York NY 10014 USA.

Lesson 55

- Students will: learn dialogue punctuation and capitalization
- Does your child remember what punctuation mark shows that someone is speaking?
    - quotation marks
    - They go around all the words the person says.
- The first letter of the quotation is capitalized.
- There is a comma either before or after the speech tag. Here are examples.
    - She said, (comma) "Please come over."
    - "Please come over, (comma)" she said.
        - The comma always comes before the quotation mark.
- The exception is if there is a question mark or exclamation point before the speech tag.
    - "Come quick!" he shouted.
    - He shouted, (comma) "Come quick!"
    - "What do you mean?" he asked.
    - He asked, (comma) "What do you mean?"
- Lesson 55 worksheet
    - They will figure out what words are being spoken first. Then they will mark that the first word of the quote needs to be capitalized and enclose the whole thing in quotation marks. Then they should check to see if there needs to be a comma after or before the speech tag.

Lesson 56

- Students will: identify syllables
- Together practice finding the number of syllables. Clap as you say each word part.
    - ball – 1
    - happy – 2
    - terrible – 3
    - toys – 1
    - giraffe – 2
    - forgetful – 3
- Lesson 56 worksheet
    - The worksheet gives them a cheat for figuring out the number of syllables in a word. If you put your hand under your chin, every time your hand goes down it's a syllable.

Lesson 57

- Students will: write a list, practice quotation marks
- Lesson 57 worksheet
  - They are to write a packing list. It's not important what they write. Correct their spelling.
  - They can use Lesson 55 for help with the quotation marks if they need it. You can also review these rules.
    - Quotation marks go around what is being said.
    - A comma goes before or after the speech tag unless there is a question mark or exclamation point.
    - All punctuation goes before the quotation mark.

Lesson 58

- Students will: identify contractions
- They are going to have to write the meanings of contractions. Here are a few to practice with. If they aren't sure, have them use the contraction in a sentence.

I'd   they've   he's   don't

  - I'd — I would
    I'd love some more. I would love some more.
  - they've — they have
  - he's — he is
  - don't — do not
- Lesson 58 worksheet
  - There are a lot. Let them know to do the ones they are sure of first and then use what they know to write similar ones. There is a lot to write for some kids.

Lesson 59

- Students will: write a descriptive story
- You can talk over the writing prompt. They are supposed to describe what they saw when visiting another country. If they can't decide, have them choose Australia. They can start with the prompt on the page, While I was visiting my friend in Australia,…
  - Have them think about what they would see and what it looked like: sizes, colors, etc.
- Lesson 59 worksheet

Lesson 60

- Students will: write a dialogue
- Lesson 60 worksheet
    - You can remind your child to look at the example on the page to remember about dialogue punctuation.
    - Each time a different person starts talking, they need to start on a new line.

Lesson 61

- Students will: practice spelling in particular with *oi, oy*, and the short "o" sound
- See if your child can think of some words with the "oy" sound and ask if they know which letters make those sounds.
    - boy – oy
    - coin – oi
- Then try to think of words with the short "o" sound as in hot.
    - pot, odd, operation, robotics
- Lesson 61 worksheet
    - They will need to count syllables and identify the short "o" sound. There's also a sentence to write.
    - They should cross out the words they've used so far and do the ones they are sure of first and then come back to the others.

Lesson 62

- Students will: write a song
- Lesson 62 worksheet
    - Encourage them to end their lines with rhymes. It can even be a song about nothing.
        - This is a song about nothing,
        - So I won't talk about anything…

Lesson 63

- Students will: review nouns and verbs
- Ask your child what a noun is.
    - a person, place, or thing
- Ask your child what a verb is.
    - an action
    - Or, it can be a word that tells someone is or something seems to be.
        - These types of verbs can be called linking verbs. They link two things together like, "This apple is delicious." If you can replace the verb with the word equal and the sentence still makes sense, then you've found a linking verb. This apple equals delicious.
    - Here are some examples of linking verbs: am, is, are, was, were, will be, has been, had been, have been, become, became
        - You can sing those to "Twinkle, Twinkle, Little Star."

- Lesson 63 worksheet
    - It's divided into sections, so they only need to look for one thing at a time.

Lesson 64

- Students will: write a friendly letter
- Lesson 64 worksheet
    - They can look back at Lesson 47 and Lesson 49 for a reminder of the format of a friendly letter.
    - Check for correct capitalization and punctuation. The salutation and closing both start with a capital letter and end with a comma.

Lesson 65

- Students will: practice punctuating sentences
- Here are a few more comma rules to introduce.
    - Put a comma between place names. (Philadelphia, Pennsylvania)
        - You can use your hometown to practice.
    - Put a comma between date names. (Friday, May 1st)
        - You can use today's date to practice.
    - Put a comma between date numbers. (March 3rd, 2015)
        - You can use your child's birthday to practice.
- Lesson 65 worksheet
    - There are a lot of corrections. They will need to look for where apostrophes go in contractions and in possessives (showing something belongs to someone).
    - There are also commas in a series and quotation marks.
    - If they are missing punctuation, give them a clue about how many more they need to find and other clues before you tell them what it is.

Lesson 66

- Students will: practice spelling, syllables, plurals, commas in a series
- Lesson 66 worksheet
    - This is a spelling worksheet. They should cross off what they have used.

Lesson 67

- Students will: write three compound sentences
- A compound sentence is two sentences combined into one.
    - It's important that each side of the sentence could stand on its own as a sentence.
    - The two sentences are connected with a conjunction. The most used conjunctions are AND, OR, and BUT.
    - Here are some examples of how to form a compound sentence.
        - I am going home, (comma) AND I will call you when I get there.
        - Please come inside, (comma) BUT please wipe your muddy feet first.
        - Do you want to play, (comma) OR do you want to rest?

- Lesson 67 worksheet
  - They have to write three sentences, and each one needs to use one of the conjunctions.
  - They should read each half of their sentence out loud to listen if it sounds like its own sentence with its own subject and verb.

Lesson 68

- Students will: be introduced to helping verbs
- Helping verbs help out other verbs. They are linking verbs that attach to action verbs.
- Here's the list of linking/helping verbs (from Lesson 63 when you maybe sang them).
  - am, is, are, was, were, will be, has been, had been, have been, become, became
  - When these verbs are used alongside action verbs, they are called "helping" verbs. Here are some examples:
    - He is coming.
    - You are going there tomorrow.
    - We had been talking nonstop for an hour.
    - I am thinking it over.
      - The highlighted verb is helping the underlined verb.
- Lesson 68 worksheet
  - This is an introduction lesson, so they just need to choose the correct one from the options.

Lesson 69

- Students will: write three compound sentences.
- You can refer to Lesson 67 for examples.
- Lesson 69 worksheet
  - They will write three sentences, each one using either AND, OR, or BUT.
  - A comma needs to come before the conjunction and both sides of the sentence need to be able to stand on their own as a sentence.

Lesson 70

- Students will: identify helping verbs and action verbs
- This has a helping verb they haven't seen yet, would. See if your child can identify what's the helping verb and the main verb.
  - I would go if I could.
  - I think he could help you with that.
    - The highlighted word is the helping verb. The underlined word is the main verb.
- Lesson 70 worksheet
  - All they need to do today is identify if the verb is a helping verb or a main verb.

Lesson 71

- Students will: practice spelling, alphabetical order, identify homophones
- Review homophones.
    - *Homo* means same. *Phone* means sound. Homophones are words that sound the same but are spelled differently. Can your child think of some?
        - pair, pear
        - meat, meet
- Lesson 71 worksheet
    - They will have to alphabetize words and find a synonym and a homophone.
    - They are to write a question as well. Make sure it ends with a question mark.

Lesson 72

- Students will: write a story with dialogue
- Lesson 72 worksheet
    - Their story is about talking with an animal or animals. They can just write the dialogue if they don't think they have a story to introduce it with.
    - Remind them to put everything said in quotation marks and to start a new line whenever someone else speaks.
        - "What do you want to do next?" I asked my dog.
        - "Sniff out a bone," he answered eagerly.
    - You can always write for them or let them type these longer writing assignments. If you write for your child, have them write at least one sentence themselves to practice putting in the punctuation and correct spelling while writing.

Lesson 73 (crayons)

- Students will: be introduced to adjectives
- An adjective is a word that describes a noun.
- Together try to think of an adjective for every letter of the alphabet. You could think of words that could describe a person. See how many you can come up with.
    - amazing, boring, careful, diligent, energetic, fake, goofy, honest, interesting,…
- Lesson 73 worksheet
    - They will identify and color in adjectives.

Lesson 74

- Students will: write a creative story
- Today's writing prompt is about a day as an inanimate object. An inanimate object is something that's not alive. Look around the room together and identify inanimate objects and think about what life would be like. Think of a pencil being held and dropped and flipped on its head and rubbed as an eraser. Think of an umbrella protecting you and getting drenched. Think of a shoe and all the things it gets into.

- Lesson 74 worksheet
  - This is a creative writing assignment, so don't worry so much about the spelling and the grammar. Let your child imagine without being constrained by being perfect.

Lesson 75

- Students will: review punctuation including apostrophes, quotation marks, and commas
- Lesson 75 worksheet
  - Let your child try it. If they get any wrong, go over that rule with them.
    - Comma after the speech tag before the quotation mark
    - Commas after each item in a series
    - Apostrophes are used in contractions and to show possession
    - Commas go between date names and numbers

Lesson 76

- Students will: practice spelling, count syllables, identify past tense
- Lesson 76 worksheet
  - This is a typical fill-in-the-blank worksheet for spelling. They will also write an exclamatory sentence (one that ends with an exclamation point).

Lesson 77

- Students will: write a creative story
- Lesson 77 worksheet
  - You could discuss the writing prompt together before they begin if you like. It's about a time they were less than an inch tall. Think together about great adjectives to describe how big things look.
    - huge, humongous, monstrous, enormous, gigantic
  - This is one you could write for your child as they dictate. The focus is on the creativity and the adjective descriptions.

Lesson 78

- Students will: choose appropriate adjectives
- Ask your child if they remember what an adjective is.
  - It's a word that describes a noun.
- Think of some adjectives together. Maybe describe things in the room.
  - white, small, smooth, hard, loud, bumpy, soft, heavy, clear, etc.
- Lesson 78 worksheet
  - They need to pick the best adjective from the choices and then fill in appropriate adjectives of their own at the bottom of the page.

Lesson 79

- Students will: write a descriptive story
- Talk over the writing prompt about a day in the woods.
    - Think of adjectives that would describe things they saw, touched, smelled, tasted, and heard.
- Lesson 79 worksheet
    - They could even write it: I spent a day in the woods and I saw….I heard…I tasted… etc.
    - Have them read it out loud when they are done and listen for mistakes.
    - This is something you might want to hang onto for their portfolio.

Lesson 80

- Students will: identify sentence types and choose appropriate ending punctuation for each sentence type
- They will have to decide if each sentence is a statement, a question, a command, or an exclamation.
    - A statement states something like this sentence: Statements end in periods.
        - Each of you think up some statements.
            - We are sitting here together.
            - Statements just tell something.
    - Questions ask questions and end in question marks.
        - Come up with questions together.
    - Exclamations exclaim and end in an exclamation point.
        - Exclaim things together.
    - Commands command, asking something or telling someone to do something. They can end in a period or exclamation point. (examples: Please help me with this. Come right now!)
        - Command each other around. Have fun.
- Lesson 80 worksheet
    - They will choose the sentence type and then correct the first letter capitalization and ending punctuation to match the sentence type.

Lesson 81

- Students will: practice spelling and alphabetical order, identify synonyms and antonyms
- Lesson 81 worksheet
    - They will follow the directions and cross off the words they have used. Review any of the directions if they are stuck; don't just give them the answer.
    - They will also write a sentence using an adjective.

Lesson 82

- Students will: write directions using ordering words
- Lesson 82 worksheet
  - Their first sentence will tell what the directions are for. They need to be directions you could really follow. It shouldn't be more than six steps.
  - Then their sentences will begin with first, second, third, etc. until the end. They can finish with "last…"
  - They need to read the directions to you and you will follow them <u>exactly</u>. Were any directions missing?

Lesson 83

- Students will: identify adjectives and antonyms
- Lesson 83 worksheet
  - They are to underline the adjective and then rewrite the sentence using the antonym of the adjective. There's a word box to help them.

Lesson 84

- Students will: write a personal narrative
- Lesson 84 worksheet
  - They will need to think of something important they have learned. You might need to help them brainstorm. How did they learn it, and why is it important?
  - They should read it out loud after they are done.

Lesson 85

- Students will: identify contractions
- Lesson 85 worksheet
  - They just need to pick the correct contraction from the choices.

Lesson 86

- Students will: practice spelling, distinguish between homophones
- Lesson 86 worksheet
  - Your child should tick off words they have used. They should realize that all of the homophone words have another word listed that sounds just like it. They need to think about which word is which.

Lesson 87

- Students will: write a descriptive story
- Lesson 87 worksheet
  - There is a picture of a tiger as a writing prompt.
  - The focus is using adjectives.

Lesson 88

- Students will: identify adjectives and synonyms
- Lesson 88 worksheet
  - They will underline the adjective in the sentence and then look for a synonym in the word box and use it to rewrite the sentence.

Lesson 89

- Students will: write a creative story
- Lesson 89 worksheet
  - The writing prompt is about a van stuffed to overflowing with bananas. The point of this is creative writing, so feel free to type or write as your child dictates the story.
  - This might be something they'd like to read aloud to others.

Lesson 90

- Students will: create compound words
- A compound word is two words combined into one. Rain and bow combine to make the word rainbow. Water and fall combine to create the word waterfall.
- Lesson 90 worksheet
  - They will match the words and then write the second half of some compound words.

Lesson 91

- Students will: practice spelling, distinguish between homophones, count syllables, identify synonyms
- Lesson 91 worksheet
  - This is a spelling worksheet. Encourage them to make their best guess about the homophones if they are unsure.

Lesson 92

- Students will: write directions
- Lesson 92 worksheet
  - They are to write the directions for how to play Simon Says. If your child doesn't know how to play, play first. ☺

Lesson 93

- Students will: use adjectives to describe a picture
- Ask your child what the adjective is in this sentence. I have one pet.
  - Numbers are adjectives.
  - One is the adjective. It describes pet.

- Lesson 93 worksheet
    - Have your child write a description of the shark and then you draw one as your child reads their description to you. Do they look alike?

Lesson 94

- Students will: write a creative story
- Lesson 94 worksheet
    - They are to continue a story they've read and tell what happened next.
    - This is one you could write as your child dictates. It's a creative exercise.

Lesson 95

- Students will: describe with adjectives
- Lesson 95 worksheet
    - They are to write five adjectives to describe each of five items in the room with them.
    - If they are stuck, you can remind your child that numbers and colors are adjectives.
    - You can reward your child with a high five and/or hug for writing more than five for one of the items.

Lesson 96

- Students will: practice spelling
- Lesson 96 worksheet
    - They will count syllables. It mentions parts of speech. So far they have learned these parts of speech: nouns, verbs, and adjectives.

Lesson 97

- Students will: write a short story starting with a character, setting, and plot
- Lesson 97 worksheet (2 pages)
    - The character of a story is who it is about. It doesn't have to be a person. It could be a dog, a robot, a superhero, etc.
    - The setting of a story is where and when it takes place. It could be the moon in 2020, the old Wild West, or the grocery store earlier today.
    - The plot is the story's action. It has to do with a problem being solved. List three problems like being allergic to your best friend, having gum stuck in your hair, or not being able to find one of your shoes.
    - Then they will write a story using one of the characters, one of the settings, and one of the problems.
        - This is one you could write or type as your child dictates.

Lesson 98

- Students will: identify adjectives and the nouns they describe
- Lesson 98 worksheet
  - They will underline the adjectives and then write the nouns they describe.

Lesson 99

- Students will: write a short story starting with a character, setting, and plot
- Lesson 99 worksheet
  - They can choose a different character, setting, and plot problem from their Lesson 97 page, or they come up with new ones.

Lesson 100

- Students will: describe nouns
- Lesson 100 worksheet
  - They are to come up with ten nouns and then the best ten adjectives they can think of. Encourage them to think of better adjectives if they choose boring ones like fun, big, sad, or just colors or numbers.
    - exciting, humongous, miserable, glittering, miniscule

Lesson 101

- Students will: practice spelling
- Lesson 101 worksheet
  - This is a spelling worksheet. They will have to count syllables, identify a synonym of probable, and words that start with a hard and soft C.
    - A hard C makes the K sound, like in the word *cat*.
    - A soft C makes the S sound, like in the word *cell*.

Lesson 102

- Students will: find the main idea and supporting details
- To practice this new concept, read this paragraph about a mongoose, named Rikki-tikki, coming to live with a family. It's from *The Jungle Book*.

  - He spent all that day roaming over the house. He nearly drowned himself in the bathtubs, put his nose into the ink on a writing table, and burned it on the end of the big man's cigar, for he climbed up in the big man's lap to see how writing was done. At nightfall he ran into Teddy's nursery to watch how kerosene lamps were lighted, and when Teddy went to bed Rikki-tikki climbed up too. But he was a restless companion, because he had to get up and attend

to every noise all through the night, and find out
what made it.

- What's the main idea? What's the paragraph about?
  - It's about how the mongoose is curious and likes to explore his surroundings.
- What are some details that support the idea that he's curious and likes to explore his surroundings?
  - He checked out every noise.
  - He roamed all over.
  - He got into the bathtub, put his nose in the ink and sniffed the cigar too close and got burned.
- Lesson 102 worksheet
  - This is what they will do. There is a short story on their page. They are to write the main idea (what it is about) in just one sentence. Then they are to list a few details that show that idea.

Lesson 103

- Students will: identify adjectives and the nouns they modify
- Lesson 103 worksheet
  - They are to underline the adjectives and write the noun they are describing. Most come directly before the noun, but some don't. It could be the furry dog or the dog that's really furry. Furry is the adjective in both cases and dog is being modified in each case.

Lesson 104

- Students will: write a postcard
- Lesson 104 worksheet
  - This is a creative writing assignment, but they can also practice letter-writing form. The person's address goes on the right. They can start with a salutation and end with a closing, making sure to capitalize them and follow them with commas.

Lesson 105

- Students will: identify prefixes, suffixes, and base words
- There are long words on their page today, and they are to find their word parts. It's best to try some examples together to explain.
  - unbelievable — *un* is the prefix, *believe* is the base word, *able* is the suffix
    - How do the prefix and suffix change the meaning of the word?
      - UN means not.
      - ABLE means able.
      - Believe turns into not able to be believed.
  - independently — *in* is the prefix, *dependent* is the base word, *ly* is the suffix
    - IN also means not. It turns dependent into not dependent.
    - LY doesn't change the meaning of the word. It changes the adjective into an adverb. It changes it from a word that describes a noun into a word that

describes an action. It's an independent person and a person who acts independently.

- Lesson 105 worksheet
  - They will write the three parts of each word in the blanks.

Lesson 106

- Students will: practice spelling, alphabetize, identify synonyms
- Lesson 106 worksheet
  - This is a spelling worksheet. They should tick off words as they use them to help them figure out the remaining words.

Lesson 107

- Students will: write a summary of a non-fiction story
- A summary is a short version of the information given. A summary should begin with the main idea. Then important facts that support the main idea should be given. If the story is about an event, the summary should include the date of the event and the names of the most important people involved. They shouldn't tell everything in the story. They need to decide what are the most important facts to include in their summary.
- Lesson 107 worksheet
  - There is a story on the page about pronghorns. They should first write the main idea, what the story was about. Then they should try to write two or three facts about that main idea.

Lesson 108

- Students will: summarize a non-fiction story
- Lesson 108 worksheet
  - They will write the main idea of the story and then two or three important facts that tell about the main idea.

Lesson 109

- Students will: summarize a story
- Lesson 109 worksheet
  - This is one of Aesop's fables, *The Fox and the Crow*.
  - They are going to summarize the story starting with the main idea of what the story is about. (It's a story of how a fox tricks a crow out of his food.)
    - Then instead of important facts, they will include two or three things that happened, telling how the fox tricked the crow. Can they tell the story in just a few sentences?

Lesson 110

- Students will: summarize a story
- Lesson 110 worksheet
  - They will summarize the story of Icarus by starting with the main idea that he died because he didn't listen to his father.
  - Then they will tell a couple of details about the story. What's important to the story?

Lesson 111

- Students will: practice spelling and writing dialogue
- Lesson 111 worksheet
  - They should tick off words as they use them to help them figure out harder ones.
  - The end of the page is two sentences with quotation marks. Check for capital letters to begin quotations and for commas to come before the quotation marks. She said, "Capital letter." "Capital letter," she said.

Lesson 112

- Students will: spell words
- Lesson 112 worksheet
  - There are pictures on the page showing the kids what words to write.
  - If your child writes duck instead of goose, don't consider it incorrect if it's spelled correctly!

Lesson 113

- Students will: write the summary of a story
- They can summarize the chapter they read today for school, or they can summarize a familiar story from a movie or favorite children's book. Before your child begins, talk about the story. What was the problem? How was it solved?
- Lesson 113 worksheet
  - Their first sentence should be the main idea. (Title) is about…

Lesson 114

- Students will: identify the main idea of paragraphs and demonstrate reading comprehension
- Lesson 114 worksheet
  - This is a multiple-choice worksheet where they will choose the main idea and answer questions about the paragraphs.

Lesson 115

- Students will: identify correct word choice for subject-verb agreement
- Lesson 115 worksheet
    - They can circle or draw a line to the correct verb choice under each noun.

Lesson 116

- Students will: practice spelling, identify contractions, alphabetize
- Lesson 116 worksheet
    - They are to put a set of words in alphabetical order and then identify the meaning of contractions. Finally, they are to write a statement and an exclamation. A statement is just a regular sentence that ends in a period.

Lesson 117

- Students will: identify the main idea of paragraphs and demonstrate reading comprehension
- Lesson 117 worksheet
    - This is a multiple-choice worksheet where they will choose the main idea and answer questions about the paragraphs.

Lesson 118

- Students will: modify nouns with adjectives
- Lesson 118 worksheet
    - They need to write in an adjective and underline the noun it modifies.

Lesson 119

- Students will: write a story summary
- Lesson 119 worksheet
    - They will summarize a story. If they aren't reading a story for school right now, they can choose any famous story to write about. They need to summarize the main idea of the story in one sentence and then include just the most important details. The summary needs to tell us the who, what, where, when, why, and how of the story.

Lesson 120

- Students will: write the correct verb to agree with the subject
- Lesson 120 worksheet
    - They will write the present tense in each blank. The present tense is what happens today. The past tense happened yesterday. The future tense is tomorrow.
        - *The babies cry* is the first one. *Cried* (past) and *will cry* (future) make sense in the blanks, but they should only use the present tense.

Lesson 121

- Students will: write comparative adjectives
- Ask your child to name some comparative adjectives.
  - Give some examples of what that means. A comparative adjective compares two things. This one is big. That one is bigger. This one is small. That one is smaller.
  - Try these:
    - hard – harder
    - tall – taller
    - beautiful – more beautiful
    - good – better
- Go over these rules of comparing adjectives.
  - If the adjective has one syllable, simply add –er to the end to make it comparative. If the word is a consonant-vowel-consonant word, you need to double the ending consonant before adding –er. If the word ends in e, simply add –r.
    - big dog – bigger dog
    - smart kid – smarter kid
    - brave hero – braver hero
  - If the adjective ends in y, change the y to an i before adding –er.
    - happy baby – happier baby
    - silly clown – sillier clown
  - For many adjectives with more than one syllable, simply add "more" to the regular adjective to make the comparative form.
    - colorful sunset – more colorful sunset
    - intelligent design – more intelligent design
    - While this is true for many adjectives, there are adjectives with more than one syllable that don't end in Y that still take the ER ending.
      - quiet – quieter
  - And of course, there are many words that just don't follow a rule.
    - far walk – farther walk
    - little time – less time
    - bad cold – worse cold
    - good show – better show
- Lesson 121 worksheet
  - They just have to write the comparative adjective. If they make a mistake, they should at least be following the rules when they do it.

Lesson 122

- Students will: identify the correct homophones and homonyms
- We've talked about homophones, words that sound the same but have a different spelling.
- Today they'll also identify homonyms, words that not only sound alike but are spelled exactly the same.
  - Can your child think of two kinds of drops?
    - a water drop and dropping something

- o Can your child think of two kinds of waves?
  - ▪ a wave in the ocean and waving goodbye
- o Those are homonyms.
- Lesson 122 worksheet
  - o This is all about identifying homonyms and homophones. With homophones the importance is in deciding which word is spelled which way.

Lesson 123

- Students will: write superlative adjectives
- Adjectives that are used to show the highest or lowest ranking among things are called superlative adjectives. Here are some rules for how they are formed.
  - o If the adjective has one syllable, simply add –est to the end to make it superlative. If the word is a consonant-vowel-consonant word, you need to double the ending consonant before adding –est. If the word ends in e, simply add –st.
    - ▪ big dog – biggest dog
    - ▪ smart kid – smartest kid
    - ▪ brave hero – bravest hero
- If the adjective ends in y, change the y to an i before adding –est.
  - o happy baby – happiest baby
  - o silly clown – silliest clown
- For many adjectives with more than one syllable, simply add "most" to the regular adjective to make the superlative form.
  - o colorful sunset – most colorful sunset
  - o intelligent design – most intelligent design
- And of course, there are many words that just don't follow a rule.
  - o far walk – farthest walk
  - o little time – least time
  - o bad cold – worst cold
  - o good show – best show
- Lesson 123 worksheet
  - o They need to write the superlative.

Lesson 124

- Students will: identify the main idea
- Lesson 124 worksheet
  - o There are short paragraphs and a choice of the main idea with one they have to write themselves.

Lesson 125

- Students will: write a story summary
- Lesson 125 worksheet
  - o They can think about a chapter they just read for school or any story they know well from a book, show, or movie. They need to summarize it. It needs to tell the

main idea and the important facts like the who, what, where, why, and how.
- o There's a challenge on the page to do it in one sentence using a conjunction. If they don't, have them look at their sentences and think about how they could combine them.
  - Example: A clownfish named Nemo was captured by a scuba diver, and his dad crossed the ocean facing many dangers to bring him safely back home.

Lesson 126

- Students will: write comparative and superlative adjectives
- You can practice a couple of these before they try it. How would they fill in the blanks? They can use any adjective. The object is to decide between the comparative (comparing two things) and the superlative (comparing many things).
  - o This is _____ than that.
  - o This is the _____ of all of them.
- Lesson 126 worksheet
  - o They can refer back to Lessons 121 and 123 for help if they are unsure.

Lesson 127

- Students will: learn the structure of a paragraph
- We've been learning about main ideas. They are often found in the first sentence of a paragraph.
  - o Open up a novel and show your child what a paragraph is. How can you tell where one ends and the next begins?
    - Each paragraph is indented.
- They are going to start writing paragraphs, and they will be taught to include the main idea as the first sentence. This can be called the topic sentence.
- Then, just like they have practiced with summarizing, they will write a couple of details that support the main idea.
- In a couple of days they will finish their paragraph with one more detail and a conclusion sentence. The conclusion tells the main idea in a different way.
- You can look at the Lesson 127 worksheet together.
  - o The hamburger picture is to help them think of the different parts of a paragraph. Today they will choose a topic and write the main idea sentence along with two supporting details.
- Here's a little example.
  - o My neighborhood is full of interesting sights and sounds. From my window I can see onto the other roofs and can watch people eat, sleep, and play on them. I hear the "eskigi" call out asking for people's old metal.
  - o My topic is about how my neighborhood is interesting. Then I tell two details about what makes it interesting.
- Lesson 127 worksheet
  - o This will be completed in Lesson 129.

Lesson 128

- Students will: identify comparative and superlative adjectives and the nouns they modify
- Lesson 128 worksheet
    - They will underline the adjectives and write the noun they modify.

Lesson 129

- Students will: write supporting details and conclusion
- They will finish their hamburger. They can just turn back and use their Lesson 127 worksheet to finish.
    - They will need to add one more detail and a conclusion. The conclusion sentence needs to mention the main idea. It needs to restate what the main idea is without just using the same sentence.
    - Here's my same example.
        - My neighborhood is full of interesting sights and sounds. From my window I can see onto the other roofs and can watch people eat, sleep and play on them. I hear the "eskigi" call out asking for people's old metal. The children play soccer in the street between passing cars. These are just some of the things that make my neighborhood interesting.
- Lesson 129 worksheet
    - They don't really need this unless they change their mind about the topic they want to do and need to start over. They are going to use their hamburger to write a paragraph in Lesson 131.
    - If your child insists they can't think of any more ideas or of how to restate the main idea, resist giving them the words.

Lesson 130

- Students will: identify the correct verb tense
- They need to find the past tense for this exercise. Here are some to practice together.
    - Yesterday he <u>flies, flew, or flown</u> to London.
        - flew
    - Last week we <u>speak, spoke, spoken</u> to them.
        - spoke
- Lesson 130 worksheet
    - They just need to choose between them.

Lesson 131

- Students will: write a paragraph
- Lesson 131 worksheet
    - They will need to copy their hamburger sentences. They should indent the first line and write their sentences all together, not one on each line.
    - You could have your child read their paragraph to an audience. You might want to photocopy it to include in your child's portfolio.

Lesson 132

- Students will: write better sentences by choosing specific nouns and verbs and adding modifiers
- Work together to make this sentence better: The dog ate.
    - Ask yourselves these questions.
        - what kind
            - What kind of dog was it?
                - a specific breed? a puppy?
                - describe it: loud, hairy, floppy, lazy,…
            - What was it doing?
                - was it chowing down, gulping, nibbling,…
        - how
            - was he eating slowly, hungrily, messily,…
            - while wiggling, while keeping an eye on the stranger, while sliding around on the tile floor,…
        - where
            - in the kitchen, the back yard,…
            - how could you describe that place?
        - why
            - because he was told to, because it was chow time, because he was starving,…
- Lesson 132 worksheet
    - They need to make the sentences better.
        - What details and interesting words can they add? How can they be more specific with the nouns and verbs?
    - If writing three sentences is going to paralyze your child, then do the first two together orally.

Lesson 133

- Students will: write a compound sentence
- Your child can make their writing better by including different sentence types. They are probably mostly writing simple sentences. A compound sentence takes two simple sentences and combines them with a comma and a conjunction such as and, or, but.
- Lesson 133 worksheet
    - They have directions on the page to write two sentences and then combine with a comma and conjunction.
    - If you want to help your child with the writing, please let them type or write out the last sentence, so they get the practice of writing the comma and conjunction.

Lesson 134

- Students will: write the parts of a paragraph
- They can use a book chapter they have just read to summarize, or if they can't think to write a summary, they can use any topic to write a paragraph.

- Lesson 134 worksheet
  - They will fill in the parts of a hamburger.
  - You can brainstorm ideas together for a topic and details.

Lesson 135

- Students will: identify the correct verb tense
- If you want to practice, here are a couple.
  - The branch had <u>fall fell fallen</u> into the road during the storm.
    - fallen
  - That's what I had always <u>think thinked thought</u>.
    - thought
- Lesson 135 worksheet
  - This practices past participles such as had fallen, have thought.

Lesson 136

- Students will: practice spelling, alphabetization
- Lesson 136 worksheet
  - They will put words in alphabetical order and find synonyms and antonyms. They should tick off words as they use them.
  - At the bottom of the page, they are to write two sentences using adjectives.

Lesson 137

- Students will: write a paragraph
- Lesson 137 worksheet
  - They just need to copy their Lesson 134 sentences into paragraph form. They should indent their paragraph to begin and start each sentence one after the other, not putting each on their own line.

Lesson 138

- Students will: identify the main idea of non-fiction paragraphs
- Lesson 138 worksheet
  - They need to identify the main idea of each short paragraph. They will choose from the options and write one main idea sentence of their own.

Lesson 139

- Students will: write a summary
- Lesson 139 worksheet
  - You could talk about the story before they begin writing. They can use a chapter they read for school today or any story from a children's book or movie.
  - They need to start with the main idea of what it was about and then choose just a few important details. The summary should tell us the who, what, where, when, why, and how.

Lesson 140

- Students will: use phonics to complete words
- Lesson 140 worksheet
  - Encourage your child to read the word with each vowel pair in the blank to listen for the correct word.
  - They should write the letters in the blank and make sure it looks and reads like a real word.

Lesson 141

- Students will: practice spelling, alphabetize words, identify synonyms, write dialogue
- Lesson 141 worksheet
  - Encourage your child to tick off words that are used to help them figure out any they are unsure of.
  - To alphabetize, they will need to look at the second letter of some of the words since they begin with the same letter.
  - When checking their dialogue, make sure that the speech tag commas come before the quotation marks. Periods and question marks will also go before the quotation mark. The first letter of each new sentence of dialogue needs to start with a capital letter.

Lesson 142

- Students will: write compound and complex sentences
- They have practiced writing compound sentences before. You can practice now as a reminder.
  - I am sitting here.
    - How could they make that sentence longer by using and, but, or and adding another sentence?
      - I am sitting here, but I really should be outside working in the garden.
      - I am sitting here, and I am reading my favorite book.
      - I am sitting here, or I'm just being lazy.
      - I am sitting here, so you'll have to find another place to sit.
        - So is one more conjunction that can be used in this way.
  - I like cold weather.
    - How could they add to that sentence with a conjunction?
      - I like cold weather, so I'm happy it's winter.
      - I like cold weather, and I'm going outside to enjoy it.
      - I like cold weather, but I will be happy when spring comes.
      - I like cold weather, or I just like fires and hot cocoa.
- They will be writing three compound sentences using and, but, or. If they really want to use so, that's okay.
- They need to write a comma before the conjunction!
- Then they will write three complex sentences.

- o These use different kinds of conjunctions. On their page, it lists for them when, if, because. Since is another one.
- o Try it together.
  - ▪ I really should be out in the garden because there's a lot of work to do.
  - ▪ I really should be out in the garden if I'm ever going to pick all those beans.
  - ▪ I really should be out in the garden when it's so nice out.
  - ▪ I really should be out in the garden since it's so nice out.
- o There is no comma before these conjunctions.
  - ▪ These are called dependent clauses. They don't need to learn the phrase. These aren't sentences on their own. I really should be out in the garden – is a sentence. We used that in our compound sentence. Because there's a lot of work to do – is not a complete sentence on its own.
- • Lesson 142 worksheet
  - o They will write three compound and three complex sentences using conjunctions. They need to change the period into a comma to make compound sentences. They need to get rid of the periods to make the complex sentences.

Lesson 143

- • Students will: identify simple, compound, and complex sentences
- • Here are some ways to identify if a sentence is simple, compound, or complex.
  - o A simple sentence has no comma. It's often shorter. It just has one subject and verb pair.
  - o A compound sentence is two sentences combined with a comma and a conjunction such as and, or, but, so.
  - o A complex sentence has two sets of subjects and verbs as well, but the one part of the sentence can't stand on its own. The two parts are connected with a different kind of conjunction such as when, if, because, since.
  - o Try some examples to practice.
    - ▪ I want to go, but I haven't finished my chores yet.
      - • compound
        - o I want to go – one sentence
        - o I haven't finished my chores yet – one sentence
        - o , but – comma conjunction
    - ▪ I will go if you come with me.
      - • complex
        - o I will go – sentence with subject and verb
        - o if you come with me – subject and verb but can't stand on its own

- If you read that on its own, it leaves you hanging. It needs some other words to go with it.
  - if – connecting word
- I will go along with Matthew, Mark, Luke, and John.
  - simple
  - one subject/verb – I will go
- Lesson 143 worksheet
  - The easiest way to tell them apart while they are still getting used to them is to look for a conjunction and to see what kind it is. Is there a comma before it?

Lesson 144

- Students will: write a simple, compound, and complex sentence
- A clause is a group of words that have a subject and verb.
- An independent clause is independent. It can stand alone and be a sentence.
- A dependent clause is dependent. It can't be alone. It depends on the rest of the sentence.
  - Because if it doesn't
    - That's a dependent clause. It needs an independent clause to help it out!
    - Because if it doesn't, then it just sounds weird.
    - It just sounds weird if it doesn't.
      - Note: there is no comma before the if, when, because, but if they start the sentence, then there is a comma after the whole phrase, the whole clause.
      - They should probably stick to using conjunctions in the middle of the sentence for now.
- Lesson 144 worksheet
  - They don't really need to get the terms independent and dependent, but they should get the concept.
  - They need to concentrate mostly on using those conjunctions properly.

Lesson 145

- Students will: write a simple, compound, and complex sentence
- Lesson 145 worksheet
  - Here's another practice page. Their compound sentences should have a comma and conjunction in between two sentences. Their complex sentences should use a different kind of conjunction without the comma.

Lesson 146

- Students will: write plurals
- Here's a reminder of plural rules.
  - For nouns ending in S, X, CH, SH, or ZZ, add –ES.
    - boss bosses
    - tax taxes
    - bush bushes

- o For nouns ending with a consonant followed by a Y, the Y changes into an I and then you add the ES.
    - baby bab<u>ies</u>
    - candy cand<u>ies</u>
  - o Most other nouns just get an S to make it plural.
    - day day<u>s</u> (vowel, Y)
    - face face<u>s</u> (S sound, not an S)
- Lesson 146 worksheet
  - o First, they'll choose the correct plural; then they will write it.

Lesson 147

- Students will: write compound and complex sentences
- Remind your child that to make a compound sentence you use a comma and a conjunction such as and, but, or to combine two sentences.
- To make a complex sentence they do not use a comma and use a conjunction such as when, if, because, since.
- Lesson 147 worksheet
  - o It is made so that they can use each conjunction one time. Encourage them to figure out where to put each so that they are each used once. Some could have more than one correct answer.

Lesson 148

- Students will: make compound and complex sentences
- Lesson 148 worksheet
  - o They are just showing understanding of the use of conjunctions. They can make their final sentence as silly as they want.

Lesson 149

- Students will: write compound and complex sentences
- Lesson 149 worksheet (2 pages)
  - o They are to write 5 simple sentences. They will have to rewrite these, so short is okay.
  - o On the second page they will use conjunctions to combine their sentences with the ones I provide. These are intended to sound silly.
  - o Check for commas before and, but, or, so, and no comma before because.

Lesson 150

- Students will: write compound sentences
- Lesson 150 worksheet
  - o They are going to write three compound sentences each using a different conjunction. Check for the comma before the conjunction.

Lesson 151

- Students will: write plurals, identify correct plural endings
- Ask your child if they want a review of the plural rules. You can use Lesson 146 in this book to go over them.
- Lesson 151 worksheet
  - There is a Bingo board. Markers may not stay on a book, so I suggest they just check off the top right corner when they get a box. You can play again and they can check off the top left corner, etc. It's up to you if you want to give them a reward for getting Bingo.
  - Here are some words to use: puppy (ies), fox (es), knife (ves), key (s), bag (s), wolf (ves), boy (s), miss (es), match (es), hero (es), elf (ves), loss (es), catch (es), baby (ies), toy (s), phone (s), party (ies), plate (s), fan (s), berry (ies), ranch (es)

Lesson 152

- Students will: write a story
- Lesson 152 worksheet
  - They are to write a story about having a pet giraffe. Give them a high five and/or hug for every sentence that uses a conjunction.
  - The point is encouraging them to use longer sentences and more variety of sentences.

Lesson 153 (red, green, blue crayons)

- Students will: identify parts of speech
- Ask your child to define nouns, action verbs, linking verbs, and adjectives.
  - Nouns: people, places, things
  - Action verbs: what someone or something does
  - Linking verbs: am, is, are, was, will, being, been,…
  - Adjectives: describe nouns
- Lesson 153 worksheet
  - If you don't have crayons to color them, come up with a key for how they will mark each part of speech.

Lesson 154

- Students will: write a story
- The plot of a story is a problem, all the things the main character does to try to solve that problem, and then how the problem is solved.
- A story is more exciting the more it seems like the problem cannot possibly be solved.
- Lesson 154 worksheet
  - They are to write a story about something being lost. Can they make it exciting?

Lesson 155

- Students will: identify correct subject/verb agreement
- Lesson 155 worksheet
  - They will choose the correct verb to agree with the subject.

Lesson 156

- Students will: review plural spelling rules, form plurals
- Singular is when there is only one. Plural is when there are more than one. These are the rules for changing singular nouns into plural nouns.
  - Usually add S.
    - computer, computers
  - Add ES to make the plural of words ending in -S, -X, -CH, -SH, -ZZ.
    - buzz, buzzes
    - bus, buses
    - church, churches
  - If a word ends with a vowel and a Y, just add S.
    - key, keys
  - If a word ends with a consonant and a Y, change the Y to an I and add ES.
    - lady, ladies
  - Some words form the plural by changing the F to V and adding ES.
    - wolf, wolves
    - shelf, shelves
    - life, lives
  - Some don't.
    - belief, beliefs
    - roof, roofs
  - Some words ending in O take an S and some ES.
    - S
      - radios
      - pianos
    - ES
      - heroes
      - potatoes
  - Some words don't follow any rule.
    - child, children
    - man, men
    - tooth, teeth
    - sheep, sheep
- Lesson 156 worksheet
  - They should do their best. Plurals of some words just need to be learned and practiced. There's no definite rule they follow. If they make a mistake, they should erase what they have and write it correctly to practice writing and reading it the correct way. They need to get used to what looks right.

Lesson 157 (optional: die)

- Students will: write a creative story
- Lesson 157 worksheet
  - There is a sort of writing prompt on the day. There are three parts of a writing prompt with three choices to mix and match in each. They can choose one from each part or they could roll a die to make the choice.
  - This is just a creative exercise, so feel free to write this out as they dictate. They could also work on typing by writing any stories like this on the computer.

Lesson 158 (red, green, blue crayons)

- Students will: identify parts of speech
- Lesson 158 worksheet
  - There are directions on the page for how to color the different parts of speech. If you don't have crayons, just come up with a key for how they are going to mark each kind. Every word is either a noun, verb, or adjective.

Lesson 159

- Students will: practice spelling
- Have a spelling bee.
  - Have your child spell the word out loud. If they get an incorrect letter, correct them until they figure it out. Then have them spell the word from the beginning again. Once they have it, they can write it on their worksheet. Then try the next word. If spelling out loud is too hard for your child, let them just write the word.
- Lesson 159 worksheet
  - Here are the words : monkeys, half, circus, flavor, apple, husband, year, celery, minute, juice, nephew, square

Lesson 160

- Students will: identify homophones
- Homophones are words that are spelled differently but sound the same. Homographs are written the same but sound differently. (You can read a book today or you had read it already yesterday.) Homonyms can be defined as words that sound the same and are written the same (baseball bat and the animal bat), but people can also use the word homonym to refer to homophones and homographs.
- Lesson 160 worksheet
  - They are to write the matching homophone/homonym in the blank.

Lesson 161

- Students will: form plurals
- Lesson 161 worksheet
  - You can ask your child if they want a review of the spelling rules. Go back to Lesson 156 in this book to review them.
  - Have them rewrite any word they get wrong.

Lesson 162

- Students will: use correct word choice
- Lesson 162 worksheet
  - Each word and word part is used only once. They need to fill in the blanks to make the sentences and stories make sense.

Lesson 163

- Students will: identify parts of speech to complete sentence structures
- Lesson 163 worksheet
  - They should fill in the blanks with a word to see what would make sense there. Is it a noun, verb, or adjective? What's the sentence missing?

Lesson 164

- Students will: write a story
- Lesson 164 worksheet
  - They are to write about a time they were brave or scared. They should think about what important details need to be in the story so that someone reading it knows the who, what, where, when, why, and how.

Lesson 165

- Students will: write a paragraph
- Lesson 165 worksheet
  - There is a writing prompt on the page.
    - How living in a cave is different from living in a house
  - They should start with a main idea sentence. (Living in a cave is very different from living in a house.) Then they can add details to explain. Then they should write a conclusion.

Lesson 166

- Students will: use phonics to complete words
- Lesson 166 worksheet
  - They need to fill in the blanks with the letters that complete the words.
  - Encourage your child to read the word out loud with the different parts if they need help figuring any out.

Lesson 167

- Students will: create characters for a play they will write
- A play is a story that is acted out. You need to think about what characters are going to be in your play.
  - You can talk about this before they put it in their workbook.
    - Who is the story going to be about? Who's the main character? Who is their friend? Their enemy?
    - They should come up with names, and they should describe each one.
      - What do they act like? Are they mean? Nice? Happy? Funny? Smart?
    - Characters don't have to be people. They can be animals or a robot.
- Lesson 167 worksheet
  - There is space for four characters. If they want more, you can give them other paper, or they can just describe them to you.

Lesson 168

- Students will: choose a setting for their play
- A setting is the where and when a story takes place.
  - They should decide where the main action of their play will take place. It can be anywhere or anytime. It could be the future or the past.
- Lesson 168 worksheet
  - They should write about their setting and can draw a picture of it too.

Lesson 169

- Students will: create a plot
- Lesson 169 worksheet
  - They need to come up with what problem their main character is going to have and how the problem is going to be solved.

Lesson 170

- Students will: organize their play
- Lesson 170 worksheet
  - They will list their main character and setting and plot problem, but they can also list other characters, settings, and problems.
  - The characters don't have to just sit in one place the whole time, and other secondary characters can be part of the story, and the more problems the main character has, the more exciting the story is.

Lesson 171

- Students will: map their plot
- Lesson 171 worksheet
  - They need to start with their problem.
  - They will think about what will create that problem or show that it's a problem. That's the beginning of the story.
  - The middle of the story is where they try to solve the problem and fail. Or maybe new problems arise. This is what makes a story interesting.
    - The more it looks like a problem can't be solved, the more exciting it is.
  - The end is where the problem is solved. How is that going to happen?

Lessons 172 through 178

- Students will: write a play
- Lessons 172-178 worksheets
  - These are just lines for writing. They should follow a format to make it easy to read.
    - The character's name on a line.
    - Then the character's words on the next line. They don't need to use quotation marks.
    - Then they can add any note about what the character is doing. Enters, leaves, lies down, jumps up and down…

Lesson 179

- Students will: revise their play
- Lesson 179 worksheet
  - They should use the worksheet to think about their play.
  - It would be good for them to read it out loud to check it for problems.

Lesson 180

- Students will: perform their play
- Lesson 180 worksheet
  - There are places for family members to comment on the play.
  - It would be fun for your child to perform the play with you and siblings, but they should at least read it out loud to an audience.
- Celebrate a great achievement! Your child wrote a play and finished Language Arts 3!

EP Language Arts 3

Workbook Answers

Lesson 2

Copywork

Copy at least three lines of poetry that are repeated in *The Lamb*, by William Blake. Write carefully and neatly.

Little lamb, who made thee?
Dost thou know who made thee,
Gave thee life, and bid thee feed
By the stream and o'er the mead;
Gave thee clothing of delight,
Softest clothing, woolly, bright;
Gave thee such a tender voice,
Making all the vales rejoice?
Little lamb, who made thee?
Dost thou know who made thee?

Little lamb, I'll tell thee;
Little lamb, I'll tell thee:
He is called by thy name,
For He calls Himself a Lamb.
He is meek, and He is mild,
He became a little child.
I a child, and thou a lamb,
We are called by His name.
Little lamb, God bless thee!
Little lamb, God bless thee!

(at least three of the following)

Little lamb, who made thee?

Dost thou know who made thee

Little lamb, I'll tell thee

Little lamb, God bless thee!

Lesson 6

Spelling

Put the <u>short a/e words</u> in alphabetical order.

batteries   every   grand

stand   vest   west

Which of the <u>other words</u> have more than one syllable?

iron   science

Which word is a **synonym** for *nigh*?   Which word is an **antonym** for *low*?

near   high

Which <u>other word</u> is plural?

forms

Write the remaining <u>other word</u>.

school

Use a <u>verb spotlight</u> verb in a sentence that ends in a question mark.

(answers will vary)

Lesson 11

Writing

Use these lines to write your poem.

(answers will vary)

Spelling

Put the <u>short i/o/u words</u> in alphabetical order.

clog   hug   inches

lunch   pond   slip

Which of the <u>other words</u> have more than one syllable?

between   country   motion

Which <u>other word</u> is plural?   Write the remaining two <u>other words</u>.

waves   yard   plant

Use a <u>verb spotlight</u> verb in a sentence that ends in an exclamation point.

(answers will vary)

Lesson 16

Writing

Write a color poem. Choose a color and write at least five lines.

(answers will vary)

Spelling

Which of the words outside of the <u>verb spotlight</u> have more than one syllable?

easy   dresses   father

value   area   matter

Which of the remaining <u>long a/long e words</u> end with a silent e?

save   grade   theme

Copy the <u>long a/e words</u> and the <u>other word</u> with a vowel pair in the middle.

sail   keep   pool

Lesson 21

Spelling

Put the long i/o words in alphabetical order.

hope	sign	stone
story	tiny	wife

Which of the other words have a sound similar to the end of *together*?

earth	current

Which word is a **synonym** for *begin*? Which word is an **antonym** for *lower*?

start	raise

Which remaining other word has a silent e to make a long vowel sound?

trade

Write the remaining other word.

else

Choose a word from the verb spotlight and use it in a sentence that ends in an exclamation point.

(answers will vary)

Lesson 23

Alphabetical Order

Put each row of words in alphabetical order by numbering the lines beside them. Sing the ABC song to yourself if you need help!

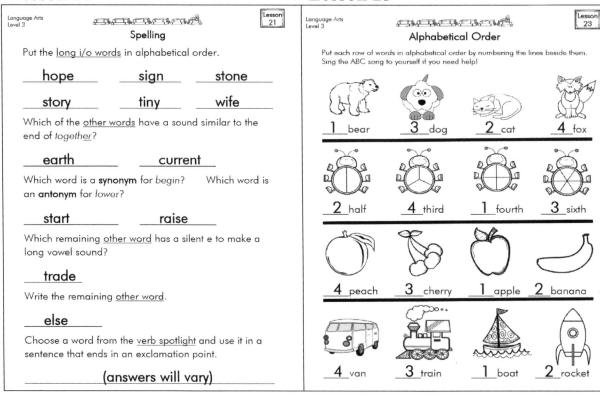

1 bear   3 dog   2 cat   4 fox

2 half   4 third   1 fourth   3 sixth

4 peach   3 cherry   1 apple   2 banana

4 van   3 train   1 boat   2 rocket

Lesson 25

Writing

Write a **moral** or a lesson. What should people know? For examples of morals, you can look at the list on lesson 22.

(answers will vary)

Alphabetical Order

Put each row of words in alphabetical order by numbering the lines beside them. Sing the ABC song to yourself if you need help!

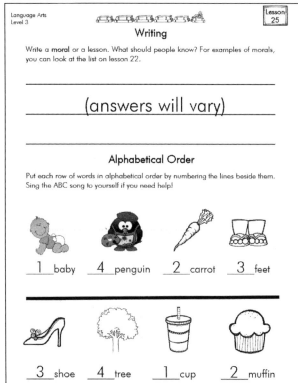

1 baby   4 penguin   2 carrot   3 feet

3 shoe   4 tree   1 cup   2 muffin

Lesson 26

Spelling

Which of the other words have more than one syllable?

upon	expand	calculate

Which of the blend words have three consonants in a row?

strong	strip	stream

burst

Which of the remaining words start with a vowel?

east	own

Put the remaining words outside of the verb spotlight in alphabetical order.

base	least	next

Use one verb spotlight verb in a sentence that ends in a period and another in a sentence that ends in a question mark.

(answers will vary)

Lesson 28

Alphabetical Order

Put each section of words in alphabetical order by numbering the lines beside them. If the first letters match, check the second letters. If the second letters match, check the third, and so on.

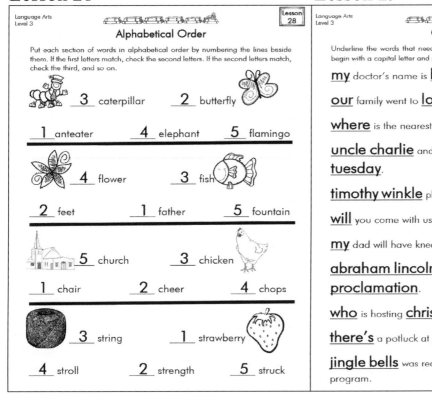

3 caterpillar   2 butterfly

1 anteater   4 elephant   5 flamingo

4 flower   3 fish

2 feet   1 father   5 fountain

5 church   3 chicken

1 chair   2 cheer   4 chops

3 string   1 strawberry

4 stroll   2 strength   5 struck

Lesson 29

Capitalization

Underline the words that need to be capitalized. Remember that all sentences begin with a capital letter and proper nouns should be capitalized.

<u>my</u> doctor's name is <u>bernadette wilson</u>.

<u>our</u> family went to <u>los angeles</u> in <u>february</u>.

<u>where</u> is the nearest <u>burger king</u>?

<u>uncle charlie</u> and <u>i</u> are going to <u>indiana</u> on <u>tuesday</u>.

<u>timothy winkle</u> plays soccer at <u>garfield park</u>.

<u>will</u> you come with us to <u>siam palace</u> for dinner?

<u>my</u> dad will have knee surgery at <u>central hospital</u>.

<u>abraham lincoln</u> signed the <u>emancipation proclamation</u>.

<u>who</u> is hosting <u>christmas</u> dinner this year?

<u>there's</u> a potluck at <u>calvary church</u> on <u>sunday</u>.

<u>jingle bells</u> was really written for a <u>thanksgiving</u> program.

Lesson 31

Spelling

Which of the <u>other words</u> are math words?

product   subtract   sum

digit   round

Which of the remaining words have a silent e?

knife   wrinkle   while

Which word is a synonym for *incorrect*?   Which is an antonym for *unknown*?

wrong   known

The two remaining words both have a silent letter. Write the words here:

knock   wrist

Use one <u>verb spotlight</u> verb in a sentence that includes a pronoun.

(answers will vary)

Lesson 32

Writing

Copy this sentence: *As he's her grandfather, it is high time he should do something for the child.*

As he's her grandfather it is high time he should do something for the child.

What is the contraction in the sentence?   What does it stand for?

he's   he is

Write another contraction here.   What does it stand for?

(answers   will vary)

Lesson 33

Comma Time

Fill in the missing commas in the lists below. Remember to add commas when you have three or more nouns, verbs, or adjectives in a row.

Is your favorite subject math, science, or history?

We went to the store, the library, and the bank yesterday.

Carrie, Scott, and Amanda went to the movie theater.

I love to run, jump, and play in the snow.

We have to shop, eat, and walk a lot in New York City.

My mom is smart, beautiful, kind, and generous.

The tall, quiet, patient doctor answered my questions.

Every man, woman, and child deserves food, shelter, and love.

The goat, the cow, and the dog all watched as the short, fluffy, black sheep tried to find the flock.

Bonus:

Tim, Jack, and Bill scrimped, saved, and hoarded their pennies, nickels, and dimes.

Lesson 36

Spelling

Which of the words outside of the <u>verb spotlight</u> have more than one syllable?

<u>enough</u>   <u>paragraph</u>   <u>photograph</u>

<u>along</u>   <u>something</u>   <u>lady</u>

Which of the <u>gh/ph words</u> are in the past tense?

<u>bought</u>   <u>laughed</u>

Which word is a homophone for *seam*?   Which is an antonym for *open*?

<u>seem</u>   <u>close</u>

Write the two remaining words that aren't in the <u>verb spotlight</u> list.

<u>graph</u>   <u>street</u>

Use one <u>verb spotlight</u> verb in a question.

<u>(answers will vary)</u>

Lesson 37

Writing

Copy these sentences. Make sure you copy them exactly. When you're finished writing them, double check that they are correct: *The strong wind nearly blew her from her seat, so she hurried with her meal, to be able to go inside and up to her bed. She slept in it as well as a prince on his royal couch.*

The strong wind nearly blew her from her seat, so she hurried with her meal, to be able to go inside and up to her bed. She slept in it as well as a prince on his royal couch.

Capitalization

Underline the words that need to be capitalized. Remember that all sentences begin with a capital letter and proper nouns should be capitalized.

<u>my</u> dad is the principal at <u>wildwood elementary</u>.

<u>the louvre</u> is a famous museum in <u>paris, france</u>.

<u>my</u> brother, <u>joey</u>, went to <u>san antonio</u> on <u>saturday</u>.

Lesson 38

Grammar Review

For each group of sentences, color in the circle next to the sentence that is written correctly. Pay special attention to capitalization and punctuation.

- ○ the bear cub came out of its den.
- ● The mother bear came out after it.
- ○ The two bears played in the sun
- ○ Then they left in search of some food?

- ● Mrs. Scott works at Lincoln Park.
- ○ Mr. Scott works at central library.
- ○ The two meet for lunch at Taco bell.
- ○ they enjoy spending the hour together.

- ○ Where did you go? asked my mother.
- ○ "I went to the playground." I answered.
- ● "I got permission from Dad," I assured her.
- ○ She noticed Dad's note on the table

- ○ I love to eat carrots, broccoli, and green beans, for dinner.
- ● My sister prefers corn, cauliflower, and squash.
- ○ My Dad is more of a meat, and potatoes kind of guy.
- ○ my mom just wants anyone else to cook!

- ○ Sylvia gave a report on glaciers
- ○ she said that she had seen some on her trip.
- ○ The class asked where she went on her trip?
- ● She told us she took a cruise to Alaska.

- ○ My dog charlie is a cute little guy.
- ○ He wags his tail whenever he sees me
- ● Charlie's favorite toy is a blue tennis ball.
- ○ He loves to run jump and roll over.

Lesson 40

Capitalization and Punctuation

Correct the sentences by underlining the words that should be capitalized and adding any missing punctuation.

We were in <u>chicago</u> on <u>sunday</u>, <u>monday</u>, and <u>tuesday</u>.

<u>the</u> three girls' dresses all matched.

My father and <u>i</u> threw, hit, and kicked the ball in the yard.

<u>she</u> wore green to the <u>saint patrick's day</u> parade.

It is so hot in <u>july</u> that I prefer to just stay inside.

<u>what</u> do you like to eat for <u>thanksgiving</u>?

<u>don't</u> touch that!

<u>my</u> scissors, glue, and paper are all over the table.

When <u>maria</u> comes home we will go to <u>café maurice</u>.

Should we wait for <u>emily</u>, <u>carrie</u>, and <u>zandra</u> to arrive?

The <u>united states</u> has a wide range of weather.

My uncle's car is in the shop until <u>friday</u>.

Lesson 41

Spelling

Put the <u>ch/tch words</u> in alphabetical order.

_____ batch _____ _____ chance _____ _____ child _____

_____ choose _____ _____ match _____ _____ watch _____

Which of the <u>other words</u> have three syllables?

_____ difference _____ _____ property _____

Which word is a synonym for *journey*? Which is an antonym for *back*?

_____ travel _____ _____ front _____

Which of the <u>other words</u> have a silent e?

_____ safe _____ _____ whole _____

Use one <u>verb spotlight</u> verb in a command.

_____ **(answers will vary)** _____

Lesson 42

Writing

Copy these sentences carefully. Check your capitalization, punctuation, and spelling: *She had gone to the housekeeper and told her all about Heidi. The lady, delighted with the idea, had told her to fetch the child at once.*

She had gone to the
housekeeper and told her all
about Heidi. The lady,
delighted with the idea, had
told her to fetch the child at
once.

Capitalization and Punctuation

Correct the sentences by underlining the words that should be capitalized and adding any missing punctuation.

<u>the</u> ball, top, and jump rope were all in the toybox.

<u>the</u> dog's name was <u>max</u>.

<u>seth</u> and <u>i</u> went to <u>southgate mall</u> yesterday.

Lesson 43

Capitalization and Punctuation

Correct the sentences by underlining the words that have capitalization errors and adding any missing punctuation. Use the clues to catch all of the mistakes.

These sentences each have 3 punctuation and 2 capitalization mistakes.

<u>the</u> boys' <u>Bathroom</u> was a dirty, disgusting, stinky mess.

My mother said that <u>carla's</u> book was under <u>jane's</u> car.

<u>Utah</u>, <u>iowa</u>, and <u>ohio</u> are shorter state names.

These sentences each have four total mistakes.

<u>can</u> you believe it's snowing in <u>october</u>?

<u>main street</u> is a block down from <u>morton avenue</u>.

My sister's favorite colors are pink, purple, and gold.

Can you find all of the mistakes without any clues?

<u>i</u> can't believe it!

<u>where</u> is the closest <u>taco bell</u>?

<u>football</u>, hockey, and rugby are some dangerous sports.

Lesson 46

Spelling

Put the <u>other words</u> in alphabetical order.

<u>children</u>   <u>fraction</u>   <u>mirror</u>

<u>ocean</u>   <u>paper</u>   <u>reflect</u>

Which <u>soft g words</u> have one syllable?

<u>stage</u>   <u>badge</u>

Which <u>soft g words</u> have a *short e* sound?

<u>gentle</u>   <u>engine</u>

Which remaining <u>soft g word</u> has a silent e that does *not* make the vowel sound long?

<u>giraffe</u>

Write the remaining word from the <u>soft g words</u> list.

<u>ginger</u>

Use a <u>verb spotlight</u> verb in a sentence that ends in an exclamation point.

_____ **(answers will vary)**

Lesson 47

Friendly Letter

Correct the friendly letter by choosing the proper correction for the bold portions.

HEADING - SALUTATION - BODY - CLOSING - SIGNATURE

November 30 2050
(a) November 30, 2050
b. November, 30 2050
c. November 30 2050.
d. November 30, 2050.

Dear Mr Hinkle,
a. Dear Mr. Hinkle
b. Dear Mr Hinkle
(c) Dear Mr. Hinkle,
d. Dear, Mr. Hinkle

Thank you for allowing me to come to your home for **thanksgiving** this year. I had a great time with your family.
a. thanksgiving,
(b) Thanksgiving
c. Thanksgiving,
d. thanks giving

Do you have any plans for Christmas? I will be spending it with my grandparents in **Los angeles, C.A.**, this year. I don't think I will be seeing any snow!
a. los angeles, C.A.
b. Los Angeles C.A.
c. Los angeles, CA
(d) Los Angeles, CA

I wish you a wonderful holiday season! Please tell your family that I said hello.

Yours Truly,
(a.) Yours truly,
b. Yours Truly
c. yours truly,
d. Yours truly:

Michael

Lesson 48

Proofreading

Correct the sentences using the clues given. Underline the answer or write the correct word in the blank to fix the mistake.

Me and Samantha enjoy the library.
Samantha and I/Samantha and me)

My mom am the driver that takes us there.
(are/**is**)

It is full of fun books for Samantha and I to take home.
(I and Samantha/**Samantha and me**)

We likes to look at the illustrations in the books.
(Make sure the verb matches the subject.)
like

Yesterday we write our own stories.
(Make sure the tense matches throughout the sentence.)
wrote

See if you can correct these sentences without any clues.

Does you have your own library card?
Do

What are your favorite kinds of book?
books

Do you enjoy pictures like Samantha and I?
me

Lesson 50

Prefixes and Suffixes

Match the prefix or suffix with the correct root word by underlining your choice.

mis____	**judge**	yard	water	room
in____	shirt	wall	**side**	color
dis____	up	down	watch	**appear**
pre____	bang	here	joke	**flight**
un____	cape	tiny	**cover**	drink
il____	floor	**legal**	skip	back
____able	chair	high	**love**	was
____ly	jump	**quick**	couch	bonus
____ing	**stand**	dog	over	pretty
____logy	shoe	brown	**bio**	hour
____er	car	flight	star	**teach**
____ness	check	**bald**	kiss	run

Lesson 51

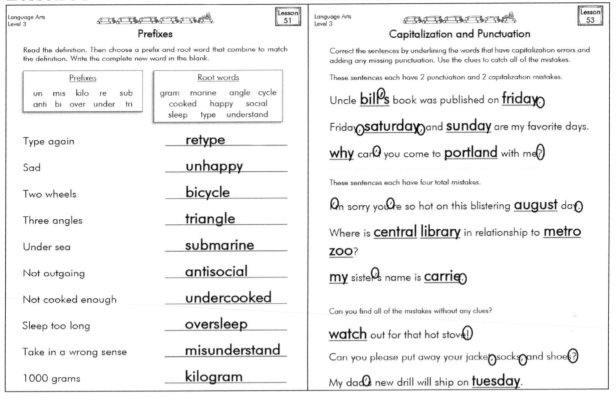

Prefixes

Lesson 51

Read the definition. Then choose a prefix and root word that combine to match the definition. Write the complete new word in the blank.

Prefixes
un mis kilo re sub
anti bi over under tri

Root words
gram marine angle cycle
cooked happy social
sleep type understand

Type again	retype
Sad	unhappy
Two wheels	bicycle
Three angles	triangle
Under sea	submarine
Not outgoing	antisocial
Not cooked enough	undercooked
Sleep too long	oversleep
Take in a wrong sense	misunderstand
1000 grams	kilogram

Lesson 53

Capitalization and Punctuation

Lesson 53

Correct the sentences by underlining the words that have capitalization errors and adding any missing punctuation. Use the clues to catch all of the mistakes.

These sentences each have 2 punctuation and 2 capitalization mistakes.

Uncle bill's book was published on friday.

Friday, saturday, and sunday are my favorite days.

why can't you come to portland with me?

These sentences each have four total mistakes.

I'm sorry you're so hot on this blistering august day.

Where is central library in relationship to metro zoo?

my sister's name is carrie.

Can you find all of the mistakes without any clues?

watch out for that hot stove!

Can you please put away your jacket, socks, and shoes?

My dad's new drill will ship on tuesday.

Lesson 55

Quotation Marks

Lesson 55

Add the missing punctuation to the sentences below by writing it in. Underline any words that should be capitalized that aren't.

"Will you come with me to the store?" asked Grandma.

"We need to get some bread and milk," she said.

Then she added, "I hope they aren't out of the things we need."

"Oh no! what will we do if they are?" she worried.

I said, "calm down, Grandma. we will just try another store."

"Of course you're right, dear," she admitted.

She continued, "sometimes I forget there are stores on every corner now."

"When I was a little girl we got everything from one general store. If they were out of what we needed we had to wait for them to order it," she explained.

"I love your stories, Grandma. now let's go get that bread and milk. I'm ready for your famous French toast!" I exclaimed.

Lesson 56

Syllables

Lesson 56

How many syllables are in the following words? Write the number of syllables in the blank beside the word. If you need help, put your hand under your chin and say the word out loud. The number of times your hand goes down is the number of syllables in the word.

caterpillar	4	bird	1
ladybug	3	apple	2
cupcake	2	bow	1
baseball	2	nest	1
butterfly	3	pencil	2
sailboat	2	carrot	2
balloon	2	basket	2
bicycle	3	egg	1
flower	2	cereal	3
baby	2	fox	1

Lesson 57

Writing

Think of a friend or relative you could visit. Write a packing list. What would you need to bring (would it be cold or warm)? What would you bring as gifts? Write ten things on your list.

1. _____   2. _____
3. _____   4. _____
5. _____   6. _____
7. _____   8. _____
9. _____   10. _____

Quotation Marks

Add the missing punctuation to the sentences below by writing it in.

"Will you please keep your voice down?" asked the librarian.

The doctor said, "I need to look in your ears now."

My sister screamed, "Ahhhhh!" as she flew down the hill on her bike.

Lesson 58

Contractions

Write what each contraction means in the blank beside it. If you're stuck, try using the contraction in a sentence and figure out what it means that way.

aren't	**are not**	you'd	**you would**
can't	**can not**	we'll	**we will**
they've	**they have**	it's	**it is**
I'd	**I would**	they're	**they are**
haven't	**have not**	I'm	**I am**
won't	**will not**	isn't	**is not**
shouldn't	**should not**	it'll	**it will**
you're	**you are**	we'd	**we would**
she'll	**she will**	wouldn't	**would not**
you've	**you have**	he'll	**he will**

Lesson 61

Spelling

Which oi sound words have more than one syllable?

___royal___   ___annoy___   ___destroy___

Which oi sound words have a silent e?

___choice___   ___voice___   ___noise___

Which other words have a short o sound?

___oddly___   ___otter___

Which other words have a different o sound?

___group___   ___forest___

Which other word is an antonym for day?

___night___

Which other word helps you solve a math problem?

___equation___

Use a verb spotlight verb in a sentence that contains a quotation.

_____ (answers will vary)

Lesson 63

Noun and Verb Review

Review your nouns and verbs. Remember that nouns are people, places, things, and ideas. Verbs show action or a state of being.

Underline the nouns in the following sentences.

The **game** we played yesterday was fun.

The **children** are yelling loudly!

Our **library** is big and quiet.

Will your **mother** be back soon?

Underline the verbs showing action in the following sentences.

The game we **played** yesterday was fun.

The children are **yelling** loudly!

Underline the verbs showing a state of being in the following sentences.

Our library **is** big and quiet.

Will your mother **be** back soon?

.Lesson 65

Punctuation

Fill in the missing punctuation from each of the sentences.

My sister's doll was left outside and it got wet, muddy, and gross.

The three boys' shoes were stinky after a day of baseball.

My dad drove us to practice and said, "We need to clean out this van."

Have you ever been to Chicago, Illinois?

Her birthday is December 20, but she celebrates it in the fall when people aren't so busy.

My dog's name is Max and her dogs' names are Sparky, Rover, and Rex.

"Watch out!" screamed my brother. "There's a snake in the yard!"

Lesson 66

Spelling

Which other words have more than one syllable?

___ desert ___   ___ important ___   ___ began ___

___ river ___   ___ influence ___

Which ou sound word is past tense?   Which ou sound word is plural?

___ shouted ___   ___ pounds ___

Which word is a synonym for ocean? Which ou sound word has three syllables?

___ sea ___   ___ however ___

Which remaining words outside of the verb spotlight have only one syllable?

___ crown ___   ___ growl ___

Write the last word outside of the verb spotlight.

___ around ___

Use a verb spotlight verb in a sentence that contains a list with commas.

___ (answers will vary) ___

Lesson 68

Helping Verbs

Circle the letter next to the helping verb that correctly completes the sentence.

Amy, Laura, and I ___ going to the mall.

(a.) are
b. is
c. am

Laura ____ asking her mom to drive us.

a. are
(b.) is
c. am

We _____ look for new shoes for our dance class.

(a.) will
b. had
c. have

I _____ hoping to find some with sparkles and a strap.

a. are
b. is
(c.) am

We _____ enjoying our dance class this year.

(a.) have been
b. has been
c. will be

Lesson 70

Main Verbs and Helping Verbs

For each sentence, tell whether the underlined verb is a main verb or a helping verb by circling your answer.

We are going to dinner for my cousin's birthday.

main verb   (helping verb)

He is turning eight years old on Saturday.

(main verb)   helping verb

My cousin loves burgers, so I'm sure we will go to a burger place.

main verb   (helping verb)

He also loves superheroes and wears a cape everywhere he goes.

(main verb)   helping verb

I hope he decides not to wear it to the restaurant.

(main verb)   helping verb

We don't need anyone tripping over his cape while carrying food!

(main verb)   helping verb

I guess that would make for a memorable evening.

main verb   (helping verb)

I love my cousin despite his silly cape.

(main verb)   helping verb

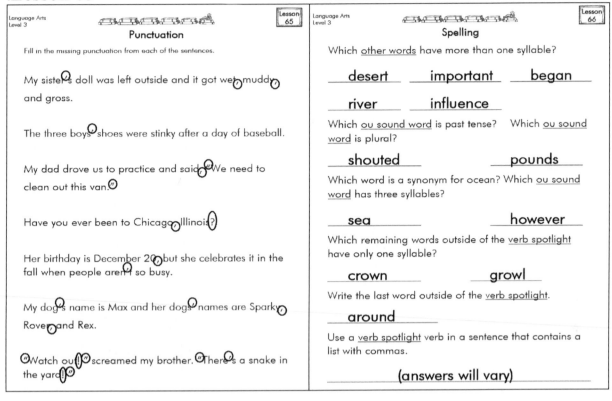

Lesson 71

Put the other words in alphabetical order.

disappear	north	once
polygon	resemble	sleep

Which two short aw words are homophones of each other?

paws	pause

Which remaining short aw words only have one vowel?

crawl	dawn

Which short aw word is a synonym for writer?

author

Write the last word that isn't a part of the verb spotlight.

laundry

Use a verb spotlight verb in a sentence that ends with a question mark.

(answers will vary)

Lesson 73

Remember that an **adjective** is a word that describes a noun. Color in the adjective flowers below.

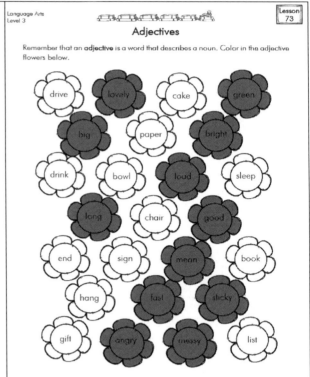

Lesson 75

Circle the letter of the option that best corrects the underlined portion of each sentence.

bill said I would love to go to the park with you tomorrow."

a. Bill said I
b. Bill said, "I
c. Bill said "I

Our library has books on dragons knights and castles.

a. dragons Knights and castles
b. dragons, knights, and, castles
c. dragons, knights, and castles

I cant find my sisters picture she made for our mom.

a. can't find my sister's
b. can't find my sisters'
c. can't find my sisters

Did you watch the news Last Night.

a. Last Night?
b. last night?
c. last night.

America's birthday is considered to be July 4 1776.

a. July 4, 1776
b. July, 4, 1776
c. July 4, 1776,

Lesson 76

Which words outside of the verb spotlight have more than one syllable?

balloon	understood	pentagon
second	predict	

Which words outside of the verb spotlight end in a silent e?

loose	goose	those

Which word is a direction?

south

Which remaining words start with the consonant blend sh?

shook	shock

Which remaining long/short oo word is past tense?

looked

Use a verb spotlight verb in a sentence that ends with an exclamation point.

(answers will vary)

Lesson 78

Adjectives

The deck was _____ after the rain. (**soaked**/scratchy)

The phone was _____ with the ringer all the way up. (purple/**loud**)

Jane's _____ blue eyes sparkled as she smiled. (angry/**beautiful**)

It was _____ news that our lost dog had returned. (**thrilling**/tasty)

The _____ painting was hanging in a museum. (**large**/energetic)

Dinner last night was _____. (bright/**delicious**)

The _____ wind blew the trees as the storm raged. (**harsh**/fluffy)

The video game was _____. (brown/**exciting**)

Write in an adjective that fits with the sentence.

Answers will vary. Examples:

The bird flew in a **straight** line.

The gravel road felt really **bumpy**.

Our **rectangular** driveway fits two cars.

The math whiz was incredibly **intelligent**.

Lesson 80

Correct the Sentences

For each sentence, choose the sentence type by circling it. Then correct the first word and add proper punctuation.

Show me how to build a snowman.

statement · ⟨**command**⟩ · question · exclamation

Where can I find some markers?

statement · command · ⟨**question**⟩ · exclamation

I can't wait for summertime!

statement · command · question · ⟨**exclamation**⟩

I'm not sure where I left my book.

⟨**statement**⟩ · command · question · exclamation

My mom is really good at organizing things.

⟨**statement**⟩ · command · question · exclamation

Please pick up your coat and hang it on the hook.

statement · ⟨**command**⟩ · question · exclamation

The sun is shining brightly outside.

⟨**statement**⟩ · command · question · exclamation

What is your favorite season?

statement · command · ⟨**question**⟩ · exclamation

Lesson 81

Spelling

Put the air sound words in alphabetical order.

airplane · **compare** · **glare**

prepare · **repair** · **stairs**

Which other word is a proper noun?

Indian

Which word is a synonym for *not quite*? Which is an antonym for *fake*?

almost · **real**

Which word has five syllables? Which word can relate to money?

quadrilateral · **buy**

Write the remaining other word.

among

Use a verb spotlight verb in a descriptive sentence with at least one adjective.

(answers will vary)

Lesson 83

Adjectives and Antonyms

This book is not short. **The book is long.**

My brother is not quiet. **My brother is loud.**

Our radio is not functional. **Our radio is broken.**

That race was not slow. **That race was fast.**

The girl is not sad. **The girl is happy.**

The man is not old. **The man is young.**

The air is not warm. **The air is cold.**

The sun is not up. **The sun is down.**

The concrete is not soft. **The concrete is hard.**

The towel is not dry. **The towel is wet.**

Lesson 85

Contractions

Choose the right bee for the flower. Which contraction correctly combines the two words?

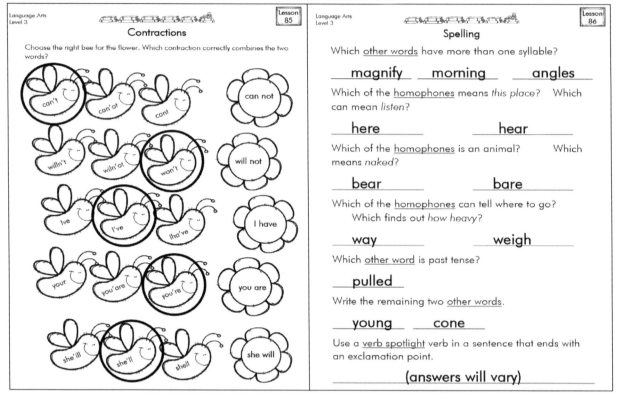

Lesson 86

Spelling

Which <u>other words</u> have more than one syllable?

__magnify__   __morning__   __angles__

Which of the <u>homophones</u> means *this place*?   Which can mean *listen*?

__here__   __hear__

Which of the <u>homophones</u> is an animal?   Which means *naked*?

__bear__   __bare__

Which of the <u>homophones</u> can tell where to go?   Which finds out *how heavy*?

__way__   __weigh__

Which <u>other word</u> is past tense?

__pulled__

Write the remaining two <u>other words</u>.

__young__   __cone__

Use a <u>verb spotlight</u> verb in a sentence that ends with an exclamation point.

__(answers will vary)__

Lesson 88

Adjectives and Synonyms

This road is <u>long</u>.   The road is **lengthy**.

My music is <u>loud</u>.   The music is **noisy**.

The road is <u>wet</u>.   The road is **soaked**.

That car was <u>fast</u>.   That car was **quick**.

The baby is <u>happy</u>.   The baby is **delighted**.

It is <u>cold</u> outside.   It is **freezing** outside.

The sandpaper is <u>rough</u>.   The sandpaper is **scratchy**.

That concert was <u>excellent</u>!   That concert was **fantastic**!

The snack was <u>yummy</u>.   The snack was **delicious**.

The <u>shiny</u> diamond sparkled.   The **glistening** diamond sparkled.

Lesson 90

Compound Words

Connect the words on the left to the words on the right to make compound words. At the bottom, make your own compound words by filling in the blanks.

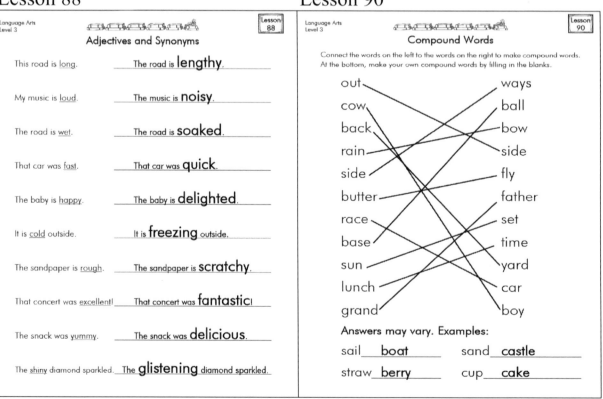

Answers may vary. Examples:

sail __boat__   sand __castle__

straw __berry__   cup __cake__

Lesson 91

Spelling

Which other words have more than one syllable?

____sugar____ ____being____ ____orbit____

____position____

Which of the homophones is a plant? Which is a bread ingredient?

____flower____ ____flour____

Which of the homophones means *uninterested*? Which is a plank of wood?

____bored____ ____board____

Which of the homophones grows on your head? Which is a rabbit?

____hair____ ____hare____

Which other word is a contraction? Which is a synonym of *depart*?

____it's____ ____leave____

Use a verb spotlight verb in a sentence that ends with an exclamation point.

____(answers will vary)____

Lesson 96

Spelling

Put the ur sound words in alphabetical order.

____church____ ____curled____ ____firm____

____perfect____ ____person____ ____skirt____

Which word has four syllables?

____experiment____

Which other words are shapes?

____polygon____ ____cylinder____

Which other words are parts of speech?

____noun____ ____verb____

Write the remaining other word.

____clear____

Use a verb spotlight verb in a question that contains adjectives.

____(answers will vary)____

Lesson 98

Adjectives and Nouns

In each sentence, underline the adjective. Then on the line beside the sentence, write the noun that is being described by the adjective.

I wore an itchy sweater to school.	sweater
My sister wants a miniature pony.	pony
The wild animals made some noise.	animals
The noisy kids sounded like animals.	kids
The delicious candy is gone.	candy
Our church has an expensive piano.	piano
The colorful robe is on the hanger.	robe
My mom has such beautiful eyes.	eyes
My aunt has long hair.	hair
The movie was boring.	movie
My brother is sick.	brother

Lesson 101

Spelling

Which double consonant words have two syllables?

____correct____ ____funny____ ____happy____

____error____

Which double consonant word has one syllable? Which has three syllables?

____hugged____ ____different____

Which other words start with a vowel?

____evidence____ ____opinion____

Which other word starts with a *hard* c? Which starts with a *soft* c?

____conduct____ ____certain____

Which word is a synonym for *probable*? Which is in the past tense?

____likely____ ____burned____

Use a verb spotlight verb in a statement.

____(answers will vary)____

Lesson 102

Summary

Read the short story by Jenn Appel below and then summarize it. Write the main idea of the story in the big oval with supporting ideas in the ovals below it.

The only thing Bristol had in mind that morning when she woke was going sledding. She rushed to do her morning chores – washing dishes, picking up her room, cleaning off the table, and starting laundry. She made quick work of all her jobs before begging her mother to go sledding.

Her mother was thrilled to see Bristol had finished all her chores without having to be told. She told her to get ready to sled. Bristol put on her snow pants, boots, coat, gloves, and hat. She grabbed her orange sled, and the two of them walked hand in hand towards the hill, both happy for the beautiful day ahead of them.

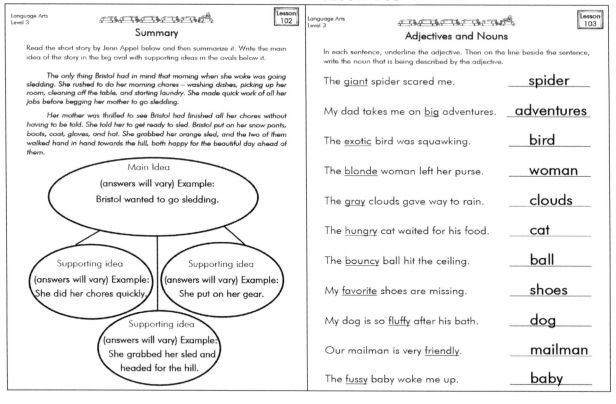

Main Idea
(answers will vary) Example:
Bristol wanted to go sledding.

Supporting idea
(answers will vary) Example:
She did her chores quickly.

Supporting idea
(answers will vary) Example:
She put on her gear.

Supporting idea
(answers will vary) Example:
She grabbed her sled and headed for the hill.

Lesson 103

Adjectives and Nouns

In each sentence, underline the adjective. Then on the line beside the sentence, write the noun that is being described by the adjective.

The <u>giant</u> spider scared me.   **spider**

My dad takes me on <u>big</u> adventures.   **adventures**

The <u>exotic</u> bird was squawking.   **bird**

The <u>blonde</u> woman left her purse.   **woman**

The <u>gray</u> clouds gave way to rain.   **clouds**

The <u>hungry</u> cat waited for his food.   **cat**

The <u>bouncy</u> ball hit the ceiling.   **ball**

My <u>favorite</u> shoes are missing.   **shoes**

My dog is so <u>fluffy</u> after his bath.   **dog**

Our mailman is very <u>friendly</u>.   **mailman**

The <u>fussy</u> baby woke me up.   **baby**

Lesson 105

Prefixes and Suffixes

Break each of the words up into prefix, base word, and suffix.

unsuccessful

Prefix: **un**   Base word: **success**   Suffix: **ful**

biweekly

Prefix: **bi**   Base word: **week**   Suffix: **ly**

unthinkable

Prefix: **un**   Base word: **think**   Suffix: **able**

insightful

Prefix: **in**   Base word: **sight**   Suffix: **ful**

misunderstanding

Prefix: **mis**   Base word: **understand**   Suffix: **ing**

inconceivable

Prefix: **in**   Base word: **conceive**   Suffix: **able**

Lesson 106

Spelling

Put the <u>compound words</u> in alphabetical order.

bookcase   **classroom**   **football**

hallway   **notebook**   **outdoors**

Which <u>other words</u> have three syllables?

conclusion   **pyramid**

Which unused <u>other word</u> is a shape? Which can be a weather word?

sphere   **forecast**

Which word is a synonym for *upcoming*? Which is a synonym for *utmost*?

future   **highest**

Use a <u>verb spotlight</u> verb in a statement and another in a question.

(answers will vary)

Lesson 111

Spelling

Which words outside of the <u>verb spotlight</u> have three syllables?

beautiful	thankfully	joyfully

helpfully	history	advantage

Which remaining words outside of the <u>verb spotlight</u> start with a vowel?

useful	until

Which word is a synonym for *happy*? Which word can mean *aspect*?

cheerful	feature

Which word can be a greeting? Which word is a container?

welcome	basket

Use a <u>verb spotlight</u> verb in a dialogue with two quotation sentences.

(answers will vary)

Lesson 112

Spelling

See if you can spell each of the words represented by the pictures below on the lines beside them.

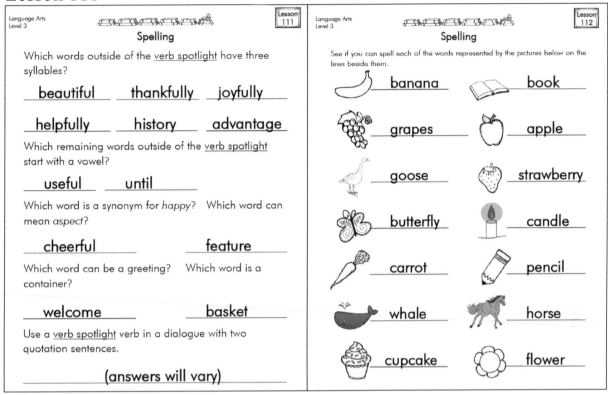

banana   book

grapes   apple

goose   strawberry

butterfly   candle

carrot   pencil

whale   horse

cupcake   flower

Lesson 114

Main Idea and Details

Read the paragraphs and answer the questions about them.

a. Sometimes main ideas are stated.

(b) Main ideas are what the paragraph or story is about.

c. Sometimes main ideas are unstated.

(a) Emma, Miley, and Kara had a fun day at the pool.

b. They played water polo while giggling and splashing.

c. They laid out in the warm sun.

a. They were glad for a day of fun in the sun.

(b) They wanted to soak up the vitamin D.

c. They wanted to have a fun day at the pool.

a. Fruits and vegetables have lots of vitamins and minerals.

b. They increase energy and leave you feeling alert.

(c) There are many benefits to fruits and vegetables.

a. They have lots of vitamins and minerals.

(b) They increase energy.

c. They can boost your immune system.

Lesson 115

Verb Vacancy

There's a verb vacancy! Help match the subjects to the correct *to be* verbs.

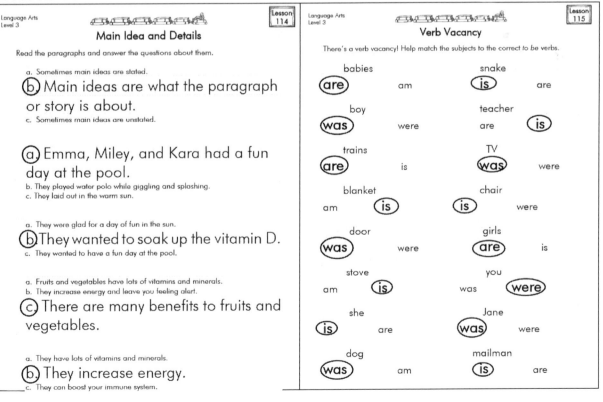

babies (are) am   snake (is) are

boy (was) were   teacher are (is)

trains (are) is   TV (was) were

blanket am (is)   chair (is) were

door (was) were   girls (are) is

stove am (is)   you was (were)

she (is) are   Jane (was) were

dog (was) am   mailman (is) are

Lesson 116

Spelling

Put the other words in alphabetical order.

climate   cycle   federal

lunar   natural   pretty

Which contractions stand for a pair of words with *not* in them?

didn't   haven't

Which contractions stand for a pair of words with *are* in them?

you're   we're   they're

Which contraction stands for a pair of words with *is* in them?

she's

Use a verb spotlight verb in an exclamation and a statement.

(answers will vary)

Lesson 117

Main Idea and Details

Read the paragraphs and answer the questions about them.

a. The colors are bright and vivid.
b. There are many plants and animals.

(c.) The jungle can be an exciting place.

a. Everyone loves the feel of sand.

(b.) I love going to the beach.

c. Salty air is refreshing.

Which of the following details supports the main idea?

(a.) The salty sea air is so refreshing.

a. Waves make a thundering sound.
b. I have sand between my toes.

a. We lose fluid that needs to be replenished.
b. Our bodies are made up of water.

(c.) Water is important for our bodies.

a. Our bodies are made up primarily of water.
b. We can survive much longer without food than without water.

(c.) We lose much fluid through evaporation, perspiration, and urination.

Lesson 118

Adjectives and Nouns

In each sentence, fill in the blank with an adjective that fits the sentence. Then underline the noun being described. **(Adjective choices will vary. Examples below).**

The shirt that I wore was **warm**.

The dishes on the counter are **clean**.

The ring on her finger was **gorgeous**.

The girl's hair was **curly**.

The cake was **gooey**.

She had **pink** gum stuck in her hair.

The **cool** water refreshed the athletes.

The **loud** crash startled them all.

His **runny** nose needs a tissue.

The cantata was **long**.

My dog looks **hungry**.

Lesson 120

Verb Vacancy

Fill in the blank with the correct *present tense* verb form of the word in parentheses. Remember that present tense words happen today.

The babies **cry** when they are hungry.
(to cry)

The snake **hisses** at the predator.
(to hiss)

The boy **plays** with his ball at the park.
(to play)

The teacher **teaches** the class with patience.
(to teach)

The trains **chug** along the tracks.
(to chug)

The TV **blares** in the next room.
(to blare)

The blanket **covers** my cold feet.
(to cover)

The chair **holds** the sitting child.
(to hold)

The girls **scream** on the roller coaster.
(to scream)

Lesson 121

Comparative Adjectives

peaceful	more peaceful	clean	cleaner
crazy	crazier	excited	more excited
young	younger	strong	stronger
angry	angrier	happy	happier
quiet	quieter	wet	wetter
green	greener	scared	more scared
big	bigger	brave	braver
bad	worse	far	farther
silly	sillier	good	better
dirty	dirtier	pretty	prettier
easy	easier	healthy	healthier
boring	more boring	friendly	friendlier
sweet	sweeter	safe	safer
high	higher	thin	thinner
busy	busier	short	shorter
large	larger	dry	drier
early	earlier	hot	hotter

Lesson 122

Homophones

Homophones are words that sound alike but have different spellings and/or meanings. For each sentence below, underline the homophone that best fits the sentence. Learn from any mistakes you make.

The ___ outside is frightful.   **weather**

___ mom is running late.   **Their**

The criminal tried to ___ the scene.   **flee**

We sang an old ___ at church.   **hymn**

Cover your eyes and don't ___.   **peek**

We ___ our bikes home.   **rode**

The story is a ___ about ponies.   **tale**

Homonyms

Homonyms are words that sound the same and have the same spelling but have different meanings. Read each sentence and fill in the homonym in the blank.

can hit a ball or fly around at night   __bat__

a group putting on a show or a hard
bandage to protect broken bones   __cast__

a type of bug or the zipper on pants   __fly__

a kind of drink or to hit with your fist   __punch__

Lesson 123

Superlative Adjectives

careful	most careful	dirty	dirtiest
scary	scariest	curious	most curious
old	oldest	cold	coldest
sad	saddest	dry	driest
long	longest	red	reddest
curly	curliest	close	closest
thin	thinnest	quiet	quietest
excited	most excited	large	largest
good	best	happy	happiest
easy	easiest	bad	worst
pretty	prettiest	busy	busiest
big	biggest	early	earliest
sweet	sweetest	far	farthest
silly	silliest	scared	most scared
brave	bravest	friendly	friendliest
high	highest	young	youngest

Lesson 124

Main Idea

Read the paragraphs and choose the main idea of each one.

(a.) Soccer is easy.
b. Soccer is fun.
c. Soccer doesn't allow hands.

a. Cockroaches don't need a lot of food.
b. Cockroaches are quick.
(c.) Cockroaches are hard to control.

a. Ladybugs are usually red.
(b.) Ladybugs come in many colors.
c. Ladybugs can be orange or yellow.

Answers will vary. Example:
Monster Trucks crush a lot of vehicles.

Lesson 126

Comparative or Superlative

My dad is _(strong)_ than yours. **stronger**

Your sister is the _(happy)_ little girl. **happiest**

Jeff is _(hungry)_ than James. **hungrier**

Canada is _(peaceful)_ than Syria. **more peaceful**

Her feet are the _(small)_ I've seen. **smallest**

My room is _(clean)_ than yours. **cleaner**

That's the _(big)_ snowball ever. **biggest**

The last clown was the _(silly)_ . **silliest**

Her hair is the _(beautiful)_ of all. **most beautiful**

The earth is _(small)_ than Jupiter. **smaller**

The swings are _(fun)_ than the slide. **more fun**

Rhode Island is the _(small)_ state. **smallest**

Her score was the _(good)_ all year. **best**

Lesson 128

Comparative and Superlative Adjectives

She was the <u>prettiest</u> girl in school. **girls**

The doll was <u>bigger</u> than the teacup. **doll/teacup**

July was the <u>hottest</u> month of the year. **months**

Friday was <u>colder</u> than Saturday. **Friday/Saturday**

The rose is the <u>most beautiful</u> flower. **flowers**

Water is <u>more beneficial</u> than soda. **water/soda**

It was the <u>longest</u> book I've ever read. **books**

Black is <u>darker</u> than pink. **black/pink**

Your car is <u>faster</u> than mine. **your car/my car**

My grandpa's car is the <u>slowest</u>. **cars**

My dog's hair is <u>fluffiest</u> after a bath. **hair**

Lesson 130

Verb Vacancy

There's a verb vacancy! Help match the subjects to the correct *past tense* verbs.

Last week, the wind (blew) blown.

Yesterday, you runned. (ran)

Last month, the door (shut.) shutted.

Last year, we helps. (helped)

A few hours ago, I drunk. (drank)

Last week, the chair (held.) holded.

Yesterday, the tree (fell.) fallen.

Last month, the boy thrown. (threw)

Last year, Jane sung. (sang)

A few hours ago, she (read) readed.

Last week, the man yell. (yelled)

Yesterday, the dog (chased) chases.

Last month, we all goed. (went)

Last year, Joseph weeped. (wept)

A few hours ago, he (came) comed.

Last week, the swing swang. (swung)

Lesson 135

Verb Vacancy

There's a verb vacancy! Fill in the blank with the correct *past participle* verbs.

The trains have ____ **gone** ____ into the station.
(went/gone)

The girl had ____ **run** ____ away from the dog.
(ran/run)

The tree had ____ **fallen** ____ in the forest.
(fallen/fell)

The wind must have ____ **blown** ____ it over.
(blown/blew)

We had ____ **drunk** ____ all the punch.
(drank/drunk)

The pitcher had ____ **thrown** ____ the ball.
(threw/thrown)

The catcher had ____ **caught** ____ it.
(caught/catched)

The boys have ____ **finished** ____ their game.
(finish/finished)

Lesson 136

Spelling

Put the other words in alphabetical order.

explorer   interaction   main

prior   state   swim

Which –er word is an antonym for *always*?   Which is a synonym for *beneath*?

never   under

Which –er word is a homophone of *weather*?   Which can mean *reply*?

whether   answer

Which –er word can indicate sickness?   Write the last –er word.

fever   border

Use a verb spotlight verb in two statements that include adjectives.

(answers will vary)

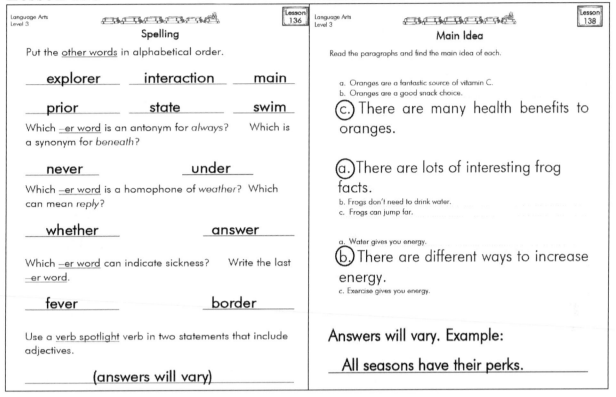

Lesson 138

Main Idea

Read the paragraphs and find the main idea of each.

a. Oranges are a fantastic source of vitamin C.
b. Oranges are a good snack choice.
(c.) There are many health benefits to oranges.

(a.) There are lots of interesting frog facts.
b. Frogs don't need to drink water.
c. Frogs can jump far.

a. Water gives you energy.
(b.) There are different ways to increase energy.
c. Exercise gives you energy.

Answers will vary. Example:

All seasons have their perks.

Lesson 140

Vowel Pairing

Use the apples to pick the vowels that are missing from each word.

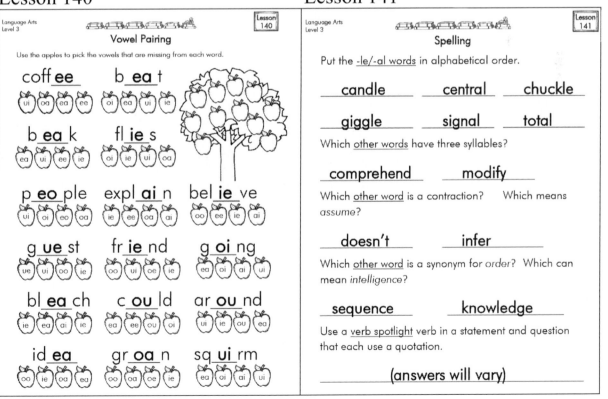

coff **ee**   b **ea** t

b **ea** k   fl **ie** s

p **eo** ple   expl **ai** n   bel **ie** ve

g **ue** st   fr **ie** nd   g **oi** ng

bl **ea** ch   c **ou** ld   ar **ou** nd

id **ea**   gr **oa** n   sq **ui** rm

Lesson 141

Spelling

Put the -le/-al words in alphabetical order.

candle   central   chuckle

giggle   signal   total

Which other words have three syllables?

comprehend   modify

Which other word is a contraction?   Which means *assume*?

doesn't   infer

Which other word is a synonym for *order*?   Which can mean *intelligence*?

sequence   knowledge

Use a verb spotlight verb in a statement and question that each use a quotation.

(answers will vary)

Lesson 143

Lesson
143

Simple, Compound, and Complex Sentences

Decide whether the following sentences are simple, compound, or complex by underlining your answer.

The bridge was crowded with cars.

simple   compound   complex

I went to the eye doctor, and he said I need glasses.

simple   **compound**   complex

You can do anything if you put your mind to it.

simple   compound   **complex**

Please park your bike in the garage.

simple   compound   complex

Her laugh was infectious.

simple   compound   complex

Put the letter in the box after you put a stamp on it.

simple   compound   **complex**

The boy, a sixth grader, was embarrassed.

simple   compound   complex

I wanted to take a nap, but I ran out of time.

simple   **compound**   complex

Lesson 146

Lesson
146

Plurals

Select the correct plural form of each word. On the next section, write each word as a plural on the blank beside it.

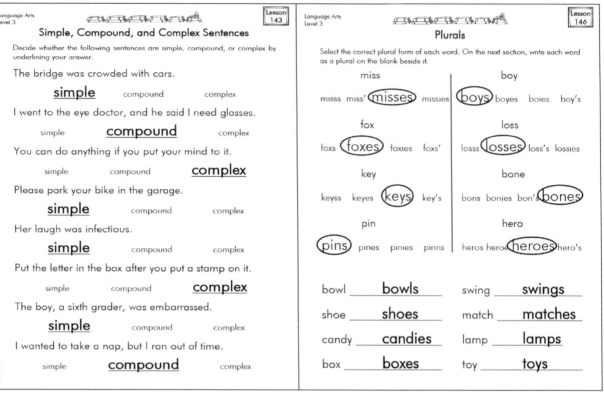

miss
misss miss' (misses) missies

boy
(boys) boyes boies boy's

fox
foxs (foxes) foxies foxs'

loss
losss (losses) loss's lossies

key
keyss keyes (keys) key's

bone
bons bonies bon's (bones)

pin
(pins) pines pinies pinns

hero
heros heroe (heroes) hero's

bowl **bowls**   swing **swings**

shoe **shoes**   match **matches**

candy **candies**   lamp **lamps**

box **boxes**   toy **toys**

Lesson 147

Lesson
147

Conjunctions

We went to the bank. Then we went to the store.

We went to the bank, (and) then we went to the store.

I like pizza. It tastes good.

I like pizza (if/because/since) it tastes good.

Wear your gloves and hat. It is cold outside.

Wear your gloves and hat (since/because/if) it is cold outside.

You can have an apple. You can have an orange.

You can have an apple, (or) you can have an orange.

She won first place. She was the best runner.

She won first place (because/since) she was the best runner.

He wished he could have gone. He was sick.

He wished he could have gone, (but) he was sick.

Lesson 148

Lesson
148

Conjunctions and Compound Sentences

Pharaoh didn't let the people go although…
(a.) God sent plagues.
b. Aaron's staff.
c. the Nile River.
d. they worked hard.

I don't want to eat that candy because…
a. I love candy.
b. too sweet.
(c.) I have a dentist appointment later today.
d. candy is delicious.

I should go to bed, but…
a. I'm tired.
(b.) I can't put my book down!
c. it's late.
d. it's cold.

I like to sing, and…
a. messy room.
b. there's a lot of trash.
c. turn the light on.
(d.) I like to dance.

Would you like to have a salad, or… **(answers will vary)**

example: would you rather have soup?

Lesson 151

Plurals

Use the grid at the top of the page as a Bingo board. The words are in the Parent's Guide. As the words are read to you, place a marker of some kind over the correct plural ending for that word. Get four in a row to win. On the bottom of the page, write the plurals of the words in the blanks beside them.

s	es	s	ies
es	ves	ies	es
ies	s	es	s
ves	es	s	ies

story __stories__   straw __straws__

paper __papers__   bowl __bowls__

turkey __turkeys__   arch __arches__

potato __potatoes__   goose __geese__

mix __mixes__   game __games__

Lesson 153

Parts of Speech

Let's review the parts of speech! Color all of the nouns blue (circled). Color all of the verbs green (x-ed). Color all of the adjectives red (untouched).

Lesson 155

Verb Vacancy

Choose the correct verb for each subject.

The cat
(was)   were

The girls
is   (are)

The laundry
have   (has)

The skates
was   (were)

I
(am)   are

The board
(has)   have

The snacks
has   (have)

The boy
(was)   were

The players
(have)   has

The game
(was)   were

The pillow
(is)   are

You
has   (have)

They
am   (are)

The toys
was   (were)

The shirt
(is)   are

The mom
(has)   have

Lesson 156

Plurals

Write the correct plurals for each of these words. Remember that some just don't follow any rules!

flake __flakes__   drop __drops__

man __men__   train __trains__

fly __flies__   mouse __mice__

mess __messes__   tomato __tomatoes__

belly __bellies__   tree __trees__

fox __foxes__   beach __beaches__

deer __deer__   glass __glasses__

radio __radios__   donkey __donkeys__

Lesson 158

Parts of Speech

Let's review the parts of speech! Color all of the nouns blue (circled). Color all of the verbs green (x-ed). Color all of the adjectives red (untouched).

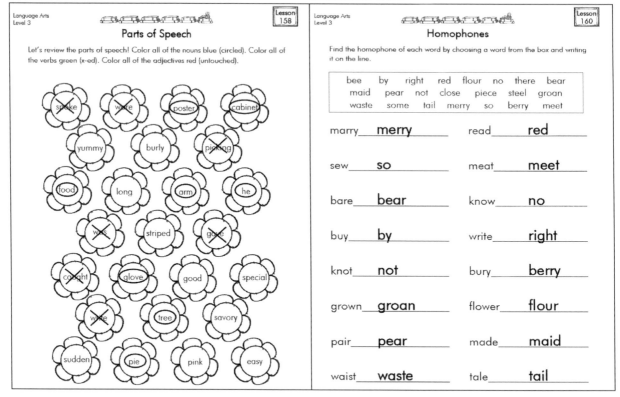

Flowers:
spoke (x), wrote (x), poster (circled), cabinet (circled)
yummy, burly, picking (x)
food (circled), long, arm (circled), he (circled)
was (x), striped, gave (x)
caught (x), glove (circled), good, special
wrote (x), tree (circled), savory
sudden, pie (circled), pink, easy

Lesson 160

Homophones

Find the homophone of each word by choosing a word from the box and writing it on the line.

bee	by	right	red	flour	no	there	bear
maid	pear	not	close	piece	steel	groan	
waste	some	tail	merry	so	berry	meet	

marry __merry__   read __red__

sew __so__   meat __meet__

bare __bear__   know __no__

buy __by__   write __right__

knot __not__   bury __berry__

grown __groan__   flower __flour__

pair __pear__   made __maid__

waist __waste__   tale __tail__

Lesson 161

Plurals

Write the correct plurals for each of these words. Remember that some just don't follow any rules!

rake __rakes__   clock __clocks__

woman __women__   giant __giants__

cry __cries__   cactus __cacti__

loss __losses__   piano __pianos__

cherry __cherries__   bee __bees__

tax __taxes__   punch __punches__

spy __spies__   class __classes__

hero __heroes__   monkey __monkeys__

Lesson 162

A Caterpillar's Voice

Circle the letter that best completes the word in the sentence.

A frightening animal was in the ___are's den.   (h) sc bl

The animal's voice ___ared out.   h sc (bl)

All of the other animals were ___ared.   h (sc) bl

Fill in the blanks with words from the word box to complete the story.

| day | cave | brave | scary |
| saving | afraid | | |

A caterpillar crawled into the hare's __cave__.

He used the echo in the cave to make himself sound

like a big, __scary__ animal. All of the other

animals were __afraid__ to go into the cave. The

frog, though, was very __brave__. He ended

up __saving__ the __day__

Lesson 163

Parts of Speech

Read the sentences below and figure out what part of speech would fill in the blank. Figure out a word that would make sense and then decide if that word is a noun, verb, or adjective.

The kids wanted to _____ before bed.

adjective   noun   **(verb)**

It takes a _____ person to accept criticism.

(adjective)   noun   verb

The _____ sang a lullaby.

adjective   **(noun)**   verb

The _____ ran down the street.

adjective   **(noun)**   verb

The dog was _____, so he ate all his dinner.

(adjective)   noun   verb

I _____ it hard to contain my excitement.

adjective   noun   **(verb)**

Lesson 166

Spelling

Choose the letters from the box that complete the words. Some of the choices are used more than once.

are	air	err	oa	ow	ou	ur	ir

c **ir** cus

ch **air**

ch **ur** ch

squ **are**

c **ow**

h **air**

cl **ou** d

b **ow**

ch **err** y

b **oa** t

Made in the USA
Columbia, SC
23 August 2020